engage

Level 3

Student Book

Alicia Artusi Gregory J. Manin

OXFORD
UNIVERSITY PRESS

CW00815876

Contents

		Grammar	Vocabulary

Remember this? *page 4*

1 Image *page 9*
- be like / look like / How + adjective
- be made of / be like
- personality
- materials and patterns

Review 1 *page 16* Study skills: Using a monolingual dictionary

2 Life issues *page 17*
- present perfect (*ever / never*)
- present perfect (*just / already / yet*)
- bad habits
- expressions with *make*

Review 2 *page 24* Reading: Little white lies

3 Foreign exchange *page 25*
- *going to* and *will*
- *might*
- travel expressions
- living overseas

Review 3 *page 32* Study skills: Learning from your mistakes

4 Creative minds *page 33*
- past progressive and simple past
- past progressive and simple past (*when*)
- sleeping and dreaming
- making things

Review 4 *page 40* Reading: A true story

5 Performing *page 41*
- comparative adjectives / (*not*) as … as
- superlative adjectives
- describing sports
- music

Review 5 *page 48* Study skills: Using word lists

6 Achievements *page 49*
- present perfect (*for / since*)
- present perfect and simple past
- business
- public activities

Review 6 *page 56* Reading: Hannah Teeter snowboard champion

7 Do the right thing *page 57*
- question tags
- *make / let / be allowed*
- travel essentials
- rules

Review 7 *page 64* Study skills: Recording vocabulary

8 Life in the future *page 65*
- *will / won't*
- first conditional
- stages of life
- the environment

Review 8 *page 72* Reading: Young people's view of the future of technology

9 A star is made *page 73*
- passive (simple present)
- passive (simple past)
- TV shows
- growing up

Review 9 *page 80* Study skills: Studying for tests

10 Relationships *page 81*
- verbs + prepositions
- infinitive or *-ing*
- relationships
- plans and opinions

Review 10 *page 88* Reading: Love in cyberspace

11 Sports world *page 89*
- indefinite pronouns
- relative clauses
- sports equipment
- sports words

Review 11 *page 96* Reading: "Game Plan"

12 Imagine *page 97*
- *would*
- second conditional
- places
- expressions with *take*, *make*, and *do*

Review 12 *page 104* Reading: What would you do to protect the enviroment?

Magazines *page 105* Puzzles and projects

Grammar summary *page 113* Irregular verb list *page 118*

Word list *page 119*

Reading	Listening	Writing	Speaking
Young and talented		Writing a profile Writing skills: Organizing information	Describing a friend Pronunciation: /u/ and /ʊ/ sounds
Star gazer	Preparing for a party Listening skills: Listening for detail	Writing an e-mail newsletter	
From Manila to Minnesota Reading skills: Paragraph topics	Planning what to do on a free day		Asking about plans Pronunciation: /iː/ and /i/ sounds
Recurring dreams Reading skills: Getting the general idea	A story about a lazy but smart dog		Talking about events in the past Pronunciation: Weak and strong forms of was and were
Try something different!		Writing about music styles Writing skills: Expressing opinions	Comparing films and TV programs Pronunciation: Word stress
Margaret Drew Reading skills: Meaning from context	A conversation about doing homework	Writing about imaginary achievements	
Style wars		Writing your own school rules Writing skills: Headings	Asking questions about people Pronunciation: Intonation in question tags
Futurology Reading skills: Subject reference	Discussing a person's future	Writing an essay about your own future	
Manufactured pop	Discussing a friend's plans to appear on TV	Describing a process Writing skills: first, then, next, after that, finally	
Signs of attraction	Three conversations about relationships		Giving news about friends Pronunciation: Responding to news
An Olympic life – Jim Thorpe (1887–1953)		Writing about sports at your school	Playing a guessing game about sports Pronunciation: /æ/ and /ʌ/ sounds
Review			

Remember this?

Travel activities

1 Match the pictures with the verbs below.
Write the correct number next to the verbs.

- 3 buy souvenirs
- ☐ carry your passport
- ☐ take a tour
- ☐ buy a ticket
- ☐ use a credit card
- ☐ drop litter

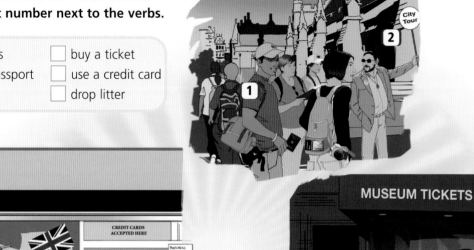

Prepositions

1 Fill in the blanks with the prepositions.

1 Greg went to Shanghai _in_ 2004.

2 The museum isn't open ___ Tuesday.

3 We go on vacation ___ the summer.

4 We're going to Florida ___ July.

5 The tour starts ___ 9 a.m.

6 The concert is ___ April 21st.

Take note!

Prepositions

in + month, year, season (**in** May, **in** 2007, **in** the spring)

on + day, date (**on** Monday, **on** January 27th)

at + time (**at** six o'clock, **at** noon)

too / not enough

1 Write sentences with *too* or *not enough* and the adjectives in parentheses.

1 Keiko's sneakers are _too big_. (big)

2 The bed is _____ . (long)

3 The beach is _____ . (far)

4 She's _____ . (tired)

5 It's _____ . (cold)

Gerunds (-ing form)

1 Write the *-ing* form of the verbs.

1 dance _dancing_   4 sit _____

2 sing _____   5 sunbathe _____

3 surf _____   6 run _____

2 Fill in the blanks with the *-ing* form of the verbs below.

dance   read   shop   snowboard

I hate (1) _shopping_ .
It's boring!

I love (2) _____ .
It's cool!

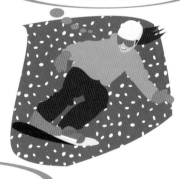

I enjoy (3) _____
science fiction books!

(4) _____
is awesome!

was / were

1 Fill in the blanks with **was** or **were**.

1 I _was_ in Argentina last summer.

2 They _____ at the movies last night.

3 A: _____ you at your friend's house yesterday evening?

   B: Yes, I _____ .

4 _____ it sunny on Tuesday?

5 Where _____ Joe on Thursday morning?

Simple past

1 Write the simple past form of the verbs in the chart.

Regular		Irregular	
1 travel	_traveled_	6 meet	_____
2 start	_____	7 have	_____
3 arrive	_____	8 go	_____
4 carry	_____	9 run	_____
5 stop	_____	10 see	_____

2 Fill in the blanks in the chart.

Affirmative	Negative
Yesterday, she (1) _went_ to school.	Yesterday, she (2) _didn't go_ to the mall.
Yesterday, we stayed at home.	Yesterday, we (3)_____ _____ at school.
Last weekend, they traveled to Panama.	Last weekend, they (4)_____ _____ to Mexico.

Question	Answer
What (5)_____ you do yesterday?	I watched TV.
Did she (6)_____ soccer last weekend?	Yes, she (7)_____ . / No, she (8)_____ .

3 Fill in the blanks in the text about Christina Aguilera. Use the simple past form of the verbs below.

be born   grow up   have   record   sign
start   win

Christina Aguilera

Christina Maria Aguilera is a singer and a songwriter. She (1) _was born_ in New York on December 18th, 1980. Christina (2)_____ in New York and Pennsylvania.

She (3)_____ her career in a TV show called *The New Mickey Mouse Club*. She (4)_____ a contract with RCA Records in 1998. In 1999, she (5)_____ an album *Christina Aguilera*. It sold eight million copies in the United States and was number one.

She (6)_____ a hit record with *Genie in a Bottle* in 1999. She (7)_____ an award at the 2000 Grammy Awards for "Best New Artist".

4 Put the words in order to make questions.

1 did / you / what / yesterday? / do

   What did you do yesterday ?

2 go swimming? / you / when / did

   _____ ?

3 they / tennis / last weekend? / did / play

   _____ ?

4 she / go / where / last week? / did

   _____ ?

5 watch TV / he / did / yesterday afternoon?

   _____ ?

Health problems

1 Match the pictures with the words below.
Write the correct number next to the words.

5 cold		☐ headache	
☐ sore throat		☐ sprained ankle	
☐ sunburn		☐ toothache	

should / shouldn't

1 Fill in the blanks with *should* or *shouldn't*.

1 A: I have a headache.

   B: You ____should____ take an aspirin.

2 A: I have a cold.

   B: You _____ go out in the rain.

3 A: I have a sprained ankle.

   B: You _____ rest your leg.

4 A: I have a sunburn.

   B: You _____ sunbathe all day.

5 A: I have a toothache.

   B: You _____ eat a lot of candy.

6 A: I have a sore throat.

   B: You _____ take a throat lozenge.

have to / can't

Take note!

We use *have to* and *can't* to talk about rules.

We **have to** wear a uniform.

We **can't** wear our own clothes to school.

1 Look at the rules of the sports club. Circle the correct word(s).

Sports Club Rules

1 You **can't** / (**have to**) wear sneakers in the gym.

2 You **have to** / **can't** use the gym on Thursday afternoon. It's closed.

3 You **have to** / **can't** speak to the receptionist about tennis classes.

4 Children under thirteen years old **can't** / **have to** swim at lunchtimes. Adults only.

5 You **have to** / **can't** put your clothes in the locker.

don't have to / can

Take note!

We use *don't have to* and *can* to talk about choices.

We **don't have to** wear a uniform.

We **can** wear what we want to school.

1 Fill in the blanks with *can* or *don't have to*.

1 You _can_ play tennis at the sports club.

2 You _____ wear white clothes to play tennis.

3 You _____ park your car in the parking lot in front of the club.

4 You _____ pay for the lessons now. Pay for the classes tomorrow.

5 You _____ use a credit card. We accept Visa or Mastercard.

have to / don't have to

Adverbs of manner

Take note!

Obligation

I **have to** clean my room.

She **has to** do her homework.

No obligation

I **don't have to** wash the dishes.

He **doesn't have to** set the table.

Take note!

add *-ly*	Irregular
quiet → quiet**ly**	hard → hard
~~y~~ + *-ily*	fast → fast
happy → happ**ily**	

1 **Fill in the blanks with *have to* or *has to* (✔) or *don't have to* or *doesn't have to* (✗).**

1 He _____ *has to* _____ take out the garbage. (✔)

2 She _____ make her bed. (✗)

3 We _____ cut the grass. (✔)

4 I _____ make lunch. (✔)

5 They _____ set the table. (✗)

6 He _____ wash the dishes. (✗)

1 **Make adverbs from the adjectives below.**

1 angry _*angrily*_   5 bad _____

2 careful _____   6 quick _____

3 good _____   7 slow _____

4 loud _____

2 **Write sentences about you. Use the adverbs from exercise 1.**

1 I eat _____ .

2 I walk _____ .

3 I play soccer / basketball _____ .

4 I do my homework _____ .

5 I sing _____ .

Review it!

1 **You need a dice. Work with a partner. Throw the dice (1–6) and answer the questions.**

How many musical instruments can you name?

Describe a classmate (physical appearance and personality). Your partner guesses who it is.

Mime a conflict verb (*argue, fight, hide* ...). Your partner guesses the verb.

Describe a sport (*you kick a ball*). Your partner guesses the sport.

How many household chores can you name?

Perform an action in the manner of an adverb (*walk quickly, talk loudly* ...). Your partner guesses the adverb.

1 Image

Grammar: *be like / look like; How + adjective / be made of / look like*
Vocabulary: personality; materials and patterns

Introducing the topic

I enjoy extreme sports.
2 _____

Do as I say!
3 _____

I feel uncomfortable when I meet new people.
1 _____shy_____

I'm the life of the party.
4 _____

I always win. I'm fantastic!
5 _____

It isn't difficult. I can do this. 6 _____

I do exercise every day.
7 _____

That shopping is heavy! Can I carry it for you? 8 _____

Vocabulary

1 Label the photos with the words below.

> arrogant   confident   daring   fit   fun
> helpful   pushy   shy

🎧 **Now listen and repeat.**

Recycling

2 Look at the photos again and find:

1 a slim girl   Photo _6_
2 a tall boy   Photo ___
3 a young girl with blond hair   Photo ___
4 a short boy   Photo ___
5 a girl with long, brown, wavy hair   Photo ___
6 a boy with long, dark, wavy hair   Photo ___

9

Exploring the topic

PEOPLE IN TV COMMERCIALS

TV commercials show different types of people. Here are some examples:

A PICTURE _2_

A girl is surfing in the sea. She's fit and daring. Her surfboard is new, she feels confident, and she's surfing well. Then she suddenly sees a big wave. The wave is coming in her direction. It's moving very quickly. She isn't ready for it. She isn't confident now. She's swimming back to the beach, but then she stops. She looks at the wave. She stands on her surfboard and she rides her surfboard to the top of the wave.

B PICTURE _____

A woman is sitting in an office. What does she look like? She's tall. She has long, wavy, red hair, and she's wearing a dark suit. What's she like? She's arrogant and pushy. She's shouting at a young man in the office. She's telling him to drive her to the station. She gets into a car and she tells him to drive fast. The young man starts the car and drives away very fast. She isn't arrogant now. She's holding on to her seat, and she's very scared.

C PICTURE _____

People are in a small club. They're friendly and fun. They're wearing cool clothes and they're listening to hip hop music. There's a new girl in the club. She doesn't have any friends with her and she looks shy. Then, a famous hip hop musician walks into the club. He's lost. He's looking for a hotel and he asks the girl for directions. Everyone stops dancing and looks at him. The girl is very helpful. She offers him a soft drink, and she gives him a map. The hip hop star thanks her. He then joins the party and raps on stage. The girl isn't shy now. She has a lot of friends at the club.

Reading

1 Read the text. Match the storylines for the commercials with the pictures.

2 🎧 Read and listen to the text. Match the commercials with the people.

1 They're friendly, fun, and confident. They wear the latest fashion, and play the latest music.
   Commercial _C_

2 She's quiet and not very confident.
   Commercial ___

3 She's healthy, lives outdoors, and enjoys exciting sports.
   Commercial ___

4 She gives orders to everyone. She thinks people should please her because she's important.
   Commercial ___

3 Which description do you think advertises:

1 a car?   Commercial _B_
2 a soft drink?   Commercial ___
3 sports clothes? Commercial ___

Grammar

be like / look like

Describing personality and appearance

1 Look at the chart.

Personality	
What **is** she **like?**	She's arrogant and pushy.

Appearance	
What **does** she **look like?**	She's tall. She has long, wavy, red hair.

2 Put the words in order to make questions.

1 does / look like? / what / he

   What does he look like ?

   He's tall and slim.

2 is / what / like / your dad?

   _____ ?

   He's fun and sometimes helpful.

3 your friends / what / like? / are

   _____ ?

   Some are shy and some are very friendly and talk a lot.

4 look like? / does / What / your best friend

   _____ ?

   He's short and blond. He has short, wavy hair and brown eyes.

5 like? / are / your teachers / what

   _____ ?

   They're friendly and helpful.

6 do / your neighbors / what / look like?

   _____ ?

   Sarah has long, straight, red hair and green eyes, and Bob is very tall.

3 Look at the profiles of the two actors. Write the questions and the answers.

1 What ___does___ Jim Carrey _look like_ ?

   _____

2 _____ is _____ ?

   _____

3 _____ does Naomi Watts _____ ?

   _____

4 _____ Naomi Watts like?

   _____

Profile
Jim Carrey – Actor
• tall, slim, dark hair
• confident and fun

Profile
Naomi Watts – Actor
• very slim, blond
• fit and friendly

Finished?
Page 105, Puzzle 1A

Over to you!

4 **Write a description of a celebrity. Can the class guess who it is?**

Appearance: He's short and slim. He has dark hair.
Personality: He's very fit and daring.
Trivia: He has a daughter.

1 Image

Building the topic

Vocabulary

1 Read the text in blue and match the people with the photos.

1 _Stew_   2 _____   3 _____

The person behind the image

Ronnie is a lawyer for a big company in São Paulo. He's a skateboarder in his free time.
Ronnie, I'm sure you love your skateboard. What's it like?
Here it is. Look. It's blue and green.
What's it made of?
It's made mostly of wood.
Now you're wearing loose jeans and patterned sneakers. What do you wear at work?
A black suit!

Raine is a bank teller in London. She also sells Goth clothes in a store in Camden Town on weekends.
Raine, tell me, what are Goth clothes like?
Well, they're mostly black. Black dresses or striped skirts, and black boots.
How long are the dresses and skirts?
They're really long – down to the floor!
You have a lot of cool accessories in your store. What are they made of?
They're made of metal and leather.
Who's the real Raine – the bank teller or the Goth?
Both.

Stew is a manager for a big corporation in New York. But after work Stew is a biker.
Hi, Stew. Now, you're a biker. Tell me, what are bikers' clothes like?
Well, we wear leather jackets, jeans, cotton T-shirts, wool hats and dark sunglasses. We also have tattoos and big metal rings.
And is this your bike? It's really cool. How fast is it?
It's very fast. It can go 250 kilometers per hour.
Now, managers look formal at work and have a nice, professional image, but bikers look rough and dangerous. What are you really like?
I'm a nicer biker than a manager.

2 Match the pictures with the words below.

1	cotton	☐	leather	☐	metal	☐	patterned
☐	plain	☐	plastic	☐	striped	☐	wood
☐	wool

 1
 2
 3
 4 5
 6
 7
 8
 9

🎧 Now listen and repeat.

3 🎧 Read and listen to the text. The <u>underlined</u> words in these sentences are incorrect. Write the correct words.

1 Ronnie wears ~~plain~~ sneakers. _patterned_

2 Stew's hats are made of <u>leather</u>. _____

3 Ronnie's skateboard is made of <u>metal</u>. _____

4 Stew's rings are made of <u>plastic</u>. _____

5 Raine wears <u>plain</u> skirts. _____

Grammar

How + adjective / be made of / be like

Describing things

1 Look at the chart.

How + adjective + *is it*?	
How long are the skirts?	They're very long.
What ... made of?	
What's it **made of**?	It's made of wool.
What ... like?	
What's your board **like**?	It's blue and green.

2 Match the questions with the answers.

1 What's your new surfboard like? _B_

2 How tall is your brother? ____

3 What's your new purse like? ____

4 What's your suitcase made of? ____

5 How heavy is this suitcase? ____

6 What's your sweater made of? ____

A It's big and it's made of leather.

B It's cool and it's really light.

C Wool.

D It's very heavy. It weighs 10 kg.

E He's very tall. He's 1.98 m.

F Strong plastic.

3 Fill in the blanks in the questions.

1 What _'s_ this bike ___made___ of?

It's made of metal.

2 What _'s_ your MP3 player _____?

It's small and light.

3 _____ your football made ___?

It's made of leather.

4 What _____ your shorts _____?

They're patterned.

5 How _____ _____ this tennis racket?

It's very light. It weighs 327g.

6 What _____ your new sneakers _____?

They're blue and white, and they're really cool.

4 Write the questions for the objects.

My computer

1 _What's it like_ _____?

It's beautiful. It has a flat screen and it's white.

2 _____?

It's not very heavy. I can carry it.

3 _____?

It's made of strong plastic and a bit of metal.

My T-shirt

4 _____?

It's black with short sleeves.

5 _____?

It cost $10. I bought it on the Internet.

6 _____?

It's made of cotton.

Finished?
Page 105, Puzzle 1B

Over to you!

5 Imagine a store window and choose two objects. Can the class guess what they are?

Student B: What's it like?

Student A: It's black with white stripes.

Student B: What's it made of?

Student A: It's made of wool.

Student B: How big is it?

Student A: It's small.

Student B: Is it a sweater?

Student A: No, it isn't. It's for your head.

Student B: Is it a hat?

Student A: Yes, it is!

Living English

Young and Talented

Danya Steele

William believes music plays an important role in our lives. After the 9/11 attacks in New York, he wanted to do something. A group of soldiers were cleaning up at Ground Zero and William played the violin for them. He played classical music for hours. The soldiers smiled and listened to William's violin in silence.

William was surprised at the power his music had on the soldiers, and started a group — Music for the People. They travel around the world, and make friends with people in other countries by playing music. William is 24 years old and lives in New York. He's a violinist, a composer, and the executive director of Music for the People.

William Harvey

Danya was the youngest chairperson ever for *HarlemLIVE*, an organisation that helps young people to become reporters, film makers, and web designers. She's also a writer, an editor, a public speaker, and a film producer. She's 22 years old and she lives in New York.

Danya writes about young people, the difficulties they have, and the news that interests them. At the moment, she's writing a book about young people who come from poor families, or don't have a family at all. It's very difficult for them to graduate from college because it's expensive. In her book, Danya says that governments should help these students because it's good for the country to have more educated people. Danya studied in Cape Town, South Africa, and at Oxford University. She's studying Social Theory and Economics in New York now.

Reading 🎧

Before you read

1 Read the article. Look at the photos. What do you think these young people do for a living?

While you read

2 Fill in the blanks with the correct name. Write *William* or *Danya*.

1 ____William____ is the founder of Music for the People.

2 _____ writes news reports and books.

3 _____ is interested in helping young people at college.

4 _____ makes friends with people around the world.

5 _____ helped soldiers in New York.

6 _____ studies in New York.

After you read

3 Read the article again and look at the photos. Answer the questions.

1 How old is Danya? *She's 22.*
2 What does she look like?
3 What is she doing now?
4 How old is William?
5 What does he look like?
6 What did he do at Ground Zero?

Writing

1 Look at the Writing skills box.

Organizing information

When you write a text, organize your information into topics.

2 Read the profile. Write the topic headings in the profile.
1 The person behind the image
2 Image
3 Looks

THE REAL JAKE

Jake is tall and slim. He has dark, brown hair. He usually wears white, cotton T-shirts, a brown, leather jacket, and a big, metal ring.

People think Jake is competitive and pushy. Girls love him, but he doesn't talk much to them. Some guys think he's arrogant and unfriendly.

Jake is very shy. He's competitive and fit because he loves sports.

3 Fill in the chart with the information about Jake.

What does Jake look like?	*tall, slim*
What do people think Jake is like?	
What's the real Jake like?	

4 Now make notes about a person you know.

5 Write the profile of the person in exercise 4. Use the text and your notes to help you.

Speaking

1 Listen and read.

2 Look at the Pronunciation box. Listen to the examples.

Pronunciation

/u/ and /ʊ/ sounds
/u/ and /ʊ/ are different sounds.

/u/ who blue
/ʊ/ look pushy

Listen again and repeat.

3 Listen to these words and write them in the correct column.

wool   wood   boots   two   group   should

/u/	/ʊ/
	wool

Listen again and repeat.

4 Practice the dialog with your partner.

5 Change the words in blue. Write a new dialog. Now practice the dialog in class.

Review 1

Vocabulary

Personality

1 Write the correct adjective.

> arrogant   confident   daring   fit   fun
> helpful   pushy   shy

1 I'm nervous about meeting new people. __shy__

2 I'm not worried about the exam. _____

3 My friends always have a good time with me. _____

4 Do as I say! _____

5 I want to go Bungee jumping. _____

6 I'm amazing. _____

7 I do the shopping for my mom. _____

8 I go to the gym every day. _____

Materials

2 Read the problem and suggest the material.

> leather   wool   wood   plastic

1 A: My school jacket is made of wool, but it gets wet in the rain.

   B: You should wear __leather__.

2 A: My suitcase is made of metal and it's heavy.

   B: You should try _____.

3 A: My surfboard is made of plastic, but it broke.

   B: You should get a surfboard made of _____.

4 A: It's winter and I'm cold in this cotton dress.

   B: You should buy a _____ dress.

Patterns

3 Replace the symbols with the correct word: *plain*, *striped* or *patterned*.

Duncan is a rapper. (1) He's wearing loose, black and white, ▮▮▮ _____ pants. (2) His T-shirt is ▬ _____. It's green with no design on it. (3) His sneakers are ▨▨▨ _____. They're very colorful.

Grammar

be like / look like

1 Write questions with *What is / are ... like?* and *What does / do ... look like?*

1 _What's Mario like_ ?

   He's very sociable and friendly.

2 _____ ?

   Rosa is slim and she has short hair.

3 _____ ?

   Sue and Kim are shy.

4 _____ ?

   Raphael is competitive and confident.

5 _____ ?

   We're tall and thin.

How + adjective / be made of / be like

3 Fill in the blanks in the questions and answers.

1 __What's__ Mario's ball like?

   __It's__ blue and striped.

2 _____ Tomiko's jacket made of?

   _____ leather.

3 How _____ your bags?

   _____ 4 kilograms each.

4 What _____ David's skateboard _____ ?

   _____ light and colorful.

2 Life issues

Grammar: present perfect (*ever* / *never*); present perfect (*just* / *already* / *yet*)
Vocabulary: bad habits; expressions with *make*

Introducing the topic

Sorry, my dog ate my homework.

Vocabulary

1 Match the pictures with the phrases below.

2 cheat on a test	☐ play a practical joke
☐ fall in love	☐ forget an appointment
☐ chew gum	☐ read someone's e-mail
☐ tell a lie	☐ write a fan letter

🎧 Now listen and repeat.

Recycling

2 Match the verbs with the irregular past participles.

1	fall	A	read
2	forget	B	been
3	read	C	told
4	tell	D	forgotten
5	write	E	fallen
6	be	F	written

3 How do you pronounce "read" in these sentences?

I always **read** in the evenings. /riːd/
I've **read** two books this month. /rɛd/

Exploring the topic

YOUR SECRET HABITS

1 Have you ever forgotten a date or appointment?
2 Have you ever chewed the same piece of gum a second time?
3 Have you ever played a practical joke on a friend?
4 Have you ever cheated on a test?
5 Have you ever told a lie to a friend?
6 Have you ever fallen in love with a stranger?
7 Have you ever read a friend's e-mail?
8 Have you ever written a fan letter to a celebrity?

A Yes, I have! I copied a friend's answers once, but they were wrong!
Xavier, Portugal

B No, I haven't. I'm just not very interested in famous people. But my sister has. She's star-crazy!
Dahlia, Tel Aviv, Israel

C I've never done it. It's a totally gross habit. My friend does it all the time. And she's chewed a piece of my second-hand gum! Eew!
Shelly, L.A., California

D I've never done it, but my sister has read mine a couple of times. I was really angry.
Wei, Harbin, China

E I've done it lots of times. Once I gave my friends some chocolate with soap in it. They didn't speak to me for days.
Annabelle, Recife, Brazil

F I've done it a couple of times. Once I told my best friend I was sick because I didn't want to play football with him.
Alfred, Stockholm, Sweden

G Yes, I have, but I'm totally embarrassed about it now. You can't love a person you've never talked to. It's just silly.
Paul, Chicago, U.S.A.

H I have, once. My boyfriend wanted to see a film with me and he was very angry.
Margaret, Vancouver, Canada

Reading

1 Read the text. Match the questions 1–8 with the comments A–H.

1 *H*   5 ___
2 ___   6 ___
3 ___   7 ___
4 ___   8 ___

2 🎧 Read and listen to the text. Write the names of the people.

1 He has fallen in love with a stranger. _____*Paul*_____
2 She missed an appointment with her boyfriend. _____
3 Her jokes have made her friends angry. _____
4 She thinks chewing used gum is digusting. _____
5 He cheated, but it didn't work. _____
6 Her sister looked at her e-mail. _____
7 She doesn't care about celebrities. _____
8 He lied to a friend because he didn't want to do something. _____

3 Which of the things have you done? What happened as a result?

Grammar

Present perfect (*ever / never*)

Talking about life experiences

1 Look at the chart.

Questions	Answers
Have I / you / we / they **ever cheated** on a test?	Yes, I **have**. / No, I **haven't**.
Has he / she **ever read** a friend's e-mail?	Yes, she **has**. / No, she **hasn't**.

Negative statements
I **have never cheated** on a test.
He **has never read** a friend's e-mail.

> ### Take note!
> The past participles of regular verbs are the same as the simple past. The past participles of irregular verbs are not the same as the simple past. There is a list on page 118.

2 Write the irregular past participles of the verbs. Look on page 118 for help.

1 be   *been*
2 do   _____
3 fly   _____
4 eat   _____
5 see   _____
6   make   _____
7   take   _____
8   go   _____
9   drive _____
10 write _____

3 Look at the pictures. Write what the people have done or have never done.

1 *She's never been ice-skating* .
(go ice-skating) ✗

2 _____
   _____
   _____ .
(eat octopus) ✔

3 _____
   _____
   _____ .
(cook a meal) ✗

4 _____
   _____
   _____ .
(fly a plane) ✗

5 _____
   _____
   _____ .
(see a lot of scary movies) ✔

4 Write the questions in the dialog with the words in parentheses.

Adrian: Let's do this questionnaire. It's called *How daring are you?* I'll ask the questions.
(1) *Have you ever driven a race car* ? (drive a race car)

Tim: No, I haven't. I'm too young to drive!

Adrian: (2) _____
_____ ? (climb a mountain)

Tim: No, I haven't, but I've been rock-climbing.

Adrian: (3) _____
_____ ? (do a bungee jump)

Tim: No, I haven't. Do you think I'm crazy?

Adrian: (4) _____
_____ ? (eat unusual food)

Tim: Yes, I have. I've eaten fried chocolate.

Adrian: Eww! (5) _____
_____ ?
(forget to do your homework)

Tim: Of course I have! Everyone has done that!

Finished?
Page 105, Puzzle 2A

> ### Over to you!
> ## 5 Write two true sentences and two false sentences about things you have done or have never done. Can the class guess the correct sentences?
>
> **Student A:** I've climbed a mountain.
> **Student B:** That isn't true.
> **Student A:** You're right.
> **Student B:** I've never written to a famous person.
> **Student A:** That's true.
> **Student B:** You're wrong. I've written fan letters to lots of people.

Building the topic

Vocabulary

1 Match the definitions with the expressions below.

- 5 make an announcement
- ☐ make a decision
- ☐ make a mistake
- ☐ make a suggestion
- ☐ make a change
- ☐ make a donation
- ☐ make a plan

1 do something wrong
2 give money or things as a gift
3 do something different
4 decide something
5 tell people some news
6 talk about a possible idea
7 plan something

Now listen and repeat.

2 Read and listen to the school magazine news page. Fill in the blanks with one or two words.

1 The writer has visited some ___colleges___ .

2 The Spring Dance organizers haven't chosen a _____ yet.

3 The bookstore has given lots of books to the _____ .

4 The cheerleaders have won _____ prize in a competition.

5 Mrs Morillo works in the school _____ .

6 The paper made a mistake about the current hours of the _____ .

---

school magazine

News shorts

READY FOR COLLEGE?

Have you seniors visited your favorite colleges and universities yet? I've already visited three universities. They're all great! I haven't made a decision on my favorite yet, but I will soon!

GETTING READY FOR THE SPRING DANCE

Have you signed up to help with the Spring Dance yet? We've just set the date. It's Saturday, April 25th. We haven't chosen a theme yet, so make your suggestions now!

GIFT TO SCHOOL LIBRARY

A local bookstore has just made a donation of 500 new books to our school library. The best part? Students can choose the books! Send your ideas to the library website.

CHEERLEADERS WIN PRIZE

The County Cheerleaders Association has just made a big announcement. Our own football cheerleading squad has won first prize in the county competition. Congratulations, cheerleaders!

SCHOOL LUNCHROOM DISASTER

Our favorite lunchroom worker, Mrs. Rosa Morillo, has just announced that she's going to retire. She says it's time for her to make a change. We'll miss you, Mrs. Morillo!

COMPUTER CENTER

We've just realized that we made a mistake in last week's school magazine. The hours for the computer center haven't changed yet. They are still 7 a.m. to 6 p.m. every day. Sorry!

Grammar

Present perfect (*just / already / yet*)

Talking about recent news and events

1 Look at the chart.

Affirmative	Negative
I've already visited three universities. A local bookstore has just made a donation.	I haven't made a decision yet.

Questions	Answers
Have you visited your favorite colleges yet?	Yes, I have. / No, I haven't.

2 Look at the pictures. Write the correct letter next to the sentences.

1   Jason has already finished the text. _A_
2   Sara has just finished the test. ___
3   David and Cass haven't finished the test yet. ___

4   Sam hasn't finished his dinner yet. ___
5   Amy has just finished her dinner. ___
6   Ben and Silvia have already finished their dinner. ___

3 Circle the correct word.

1   A: Is *Party Animal* a good movie?
    B: I haven't seen it already / yet.
2   Have you finished your history paper already / yet?
3   Juan hasn't decided which sport to play already / yet.
4   A: Is Casie going to study in New York?
    B: Yes, she's just / yet made a decision.
5   Amelie has already / yet played with an orchestra, and she's only ten!
6   Carlos hasn't started at his new school just / yet.

4 Fill in the blanks with the words in parentheses.

1   A: _Have you finished your homework yet_?
    (you / finish / homework / yet)
    B: _I've already finished_ my English homework, but I'm having trouble with math.
    (I / already / finish)
2   A: Timothy _____ the tennis competition. (just / win)
    B: That's great. _____
    _____? (he / receive / the prize / yet)
3   A: Jo and Deb _____
    _____ five concerts this month! (already / go)
    B: _____
    _____?
    (they / buy / tickets / for the concert / yet)

Finished?
Page 105, Puzzle 2B

Over to you!

5 Look at the words below. Can the class guess what has happened?

Congratulations!   Oh no!   Cool!   Help!

Student A: Congratulations!
Student B: They've just got married.
Student C: He's just graduated from high school.
Student D: She's just won a prize.

Living English

star gazer

The latest news and gossip on all your favorite stars

A Filmmaker **Nat Harmer** has just won an award for his latest film, *No Way Out.* He's already received international awards for three of his other films. He hasn't announced the name of his next film yet. It stars **Kathy Warren** and **Marty Shine**. We can't wait!

B It looks like child actor **Aaron McDarney** has already retired – and he's just 16 years old! "He's a great actor, but he's also an excellent student," says his manager. "He's just finished high school, and now he wants to go to college." His subject? Astrophysics!

C Why haven't we heard **Nina Ray's** new CD yet? Well, her record producer says there have been problems recording some of the songs. Nina has already made four CDs, but the last one came out three years ago. Come on, girl! We've already waited too long!

Nina Ray

D Everyone knows that singer **Tim Marvin** loves animals. Well, he's just started a group to help homeless reptiles. That's right! He wants to find homes for all those snakes and alligators that people have left in the wild. Tim has already collected almost a million dollars for his organization, and he's taken two large snakes and a tortoise into his home as pets.

Tim Marvin

Rose Medley

E Closer to home, we've just learned that our own writer, **Rose Medley**, has finished her first book. Is it about celebrities? Not exactly. "I've always loved history," Rose tells us. "So, I've decided to write a book about women leaders. There have always been strong women in history, but we don't know a lot about them." We can't wait to read your new book, Rose!

Reading 🎧

Before you read

1 Look at the title and the pictures. Where can you find this kind of article? What kind of people does it talk about?

While you read

2 Read the text quickly. Check (✓) the subjects that are mentioned in the text.

1 books ✓   2 movies ___   3 charities ___

4 music ___   5 college ___   6 prizes ___

7 gardening ___   8 websites ___

After you read

3 Read the text again. Match the headlines to the news reports.

1 How Long Does It Take? _C_

2 A Secret History ___

3 Lions, Tigers, and … Snakes? ___

4 Early Retirement ___

5 Another Prize-Winner ___

4 Circle T (True) or F (False).

1 Nat Harmer is an actor. T /(F)

2 The name of Nat Harmer's next project is *No Way Out.* T / F

3 Nina Ray's new CD will be out soon. T / F

4 Aaron McDarney has already finished college. T / F

5 Tim Marvin has started a charity to help certain animals. T / F

6 Rose Medley's book is about important women. T / F

Listening 🎧

1 Look at the Listening skills box.

Listening for detail

When you're listening, pay attention to the verbs.
Are they affirmative or negative?

2 **Naomi and David are planning a party. Listen to the conversation. Put a check (✓) for a *Yes* answer or a cross (✗) for a *No* answer.**

1   buy food ✗
2   make music CD
3   buy decorations
4   get prizes
5   send e-mails
6   talk to Jan's parents

3 **Listen again. Circle the correct answers.**

1   The party is in ② / 3 days.
2   Naomi has already bought the prizes / decorations.
3   David has already made the CDs / prizes.
4   David has talked to Jan's parents about sending e-mails / using their house.

Writing

1 Read the e-mail newsletter.

⊖ ○ ○

The McClure Family Newsletter

My brother James and his partner, Amelda, have just had their wedding. They haven't gone on their honeymoon yet. They plan to go to Hawaii next month. Congratulations, J and A!

My mother has just received her master's degree from the University of Utah. She did a lot of work, but now it's over, so more congratulations!

Our favorite neighbors, Jean, Sophie, Marc, and Antoine, have just moved back to France after two years in our town. We were very sad to see them go. We haven't heard from them yet, but they promised to keep in touch. Look for more updates.

One more bit of news. My brother, Tad, has just applied to study abroad. He wants to go to Japan. Good luck, Tad. And remember, we all plan to visit you while you're there!

That's all for this month!
Katie – for all the McClures

2 Fill in the chart with the information from Katie's newsletter.

Event	Comment
1 brother James has just got married	haven't gone on honeymoon yet – plan to go to Hawaii
2	
3	
4	

3 Now make notes about your family.

4 Write your newsletter. Use the text and your notes to help you.

Review 2

Vocabulary

Bad habits

1 **Fill in the blanks. Use the past participle.**

1   I've never _chewed_ gum in class.

2   Have you ever _____ an appointment?

3   Sam has _____ a practical joke on me.

4   I've _____ my sister's e-mail.

5   Ariel has _____ in love with José.

6   Have you ever _____ on a test?

7   I've never _____ a lie to my best friend.

8   Lucy has _____ a fan letter to Jude Law.

Expressions with *make*

2 **Correct the expressions with *make* in each sentence.**

1   Have you made a ~~donation~~ about what college to go to? _decision_

2   We've just made a decision of $200 to the art museum. _____

3   I got a bad grade on my test because I made a lot of suggestions. _____

4   I'm bored of my job. I need to make a mistake. _____

5   Can I make a change? Let's see a movie. _____

6   Have you made any announcements for your vacation? _____

7   Mei has just made an plan to everybody. She's getting married. _____

Grammar

Present perfect (*ever / never*)

1 **Write the questions or statements. Use the cues.**

1   you / see / a Woody Allen movie
    Have you ever seen a Woody Allen movie ?

2   we / never / go / to Disneyland
    _____ .

3   Tom / ever / tell a lie
    _____ ?

4   your dad / ever / drive / a Mercedes
    _____ ?

5   Adiva / never / study / French
    _____ .

Present perfect (*just / already / yet*)

2 **Look at the pictures. Write *just*, *yet* or *already*.**

1   The hairdresser has _already_ cut Lucy's hair.
    The hairdresser hasn't started Delia's hair _____.
    The hairdresser has _____ done Amanda's hair.

2   Lucy has _____ finished her coffee.
    Amanda hasn't drunk her coffee _____ .
    Delia has _____ drunk her coffee.

Reading

1 **Read the article and circle T (True) or F (False).**

LITTLE WHITE LIES

Are lies always wrong, or are small lies (white lies) sometimes necessary? We asked 50 young people. Most people thought lies were wrong. But they didn't all agree about what a lie really is. "I've never told my parents a real lie," says one sixteen-year-old girl. "Of course, I sometimes tell them I'm in one place when I'm in another place because I don't want them to worry."
Most young people think it's wrong to tell lies about where you are. "I've never lied to my parents," one eighteen-year-old boy says. "They need to know where I am, and who I'm with." What about telling lies to friends? "I've done it," one younger teenager says. "But the truth is always better. Friends are going to find out that you lied, and then the problems get really big."

1   All the young people think lies are wrong. T /(F)

2   They have different ideas about what a lie is. T / F

3   The girl never tells white lies. T / F

4   The boy thinks parents need to know the truth. T / F

5   The last teenager thinks lying is a bad idea. T / F

3 Foreign exchange

Grammar: *going to* and *will*; *might*
Vocabulary: travel expressions; living overseas

Introducing the topic

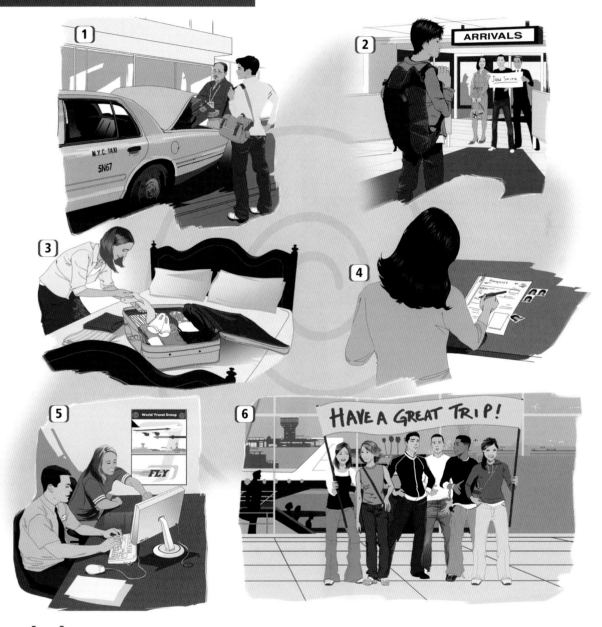

Vocabulary

1 Match the pictures with the phrases below.

- [4] apply for a passport
- [ ] pack your bags
- [ ] see someone off
- [ ] book a flight
- [ ] pick someone up
- [ ] take a taxi

🎧 **Now listen and repeat.**

Recycling

2 Look at the list of objects. Check (✓) the ones you usually take on vacation.

- [ ] backpack
- [ ] homework
- [ ] magazine
- [ ] camera
- [ ] suitcase
- [ ] diary
- [ ] computer
- [ ] MP3 player
- [ ] cellphone

Exploring the topic

TRIP TO JAPAN

JAPAN
High School Exchange

Study in a Japanese school!
Live with a Japanese family!
Learn about Japan!
Make new friends!

Question 1 I'm going to apply for my passport in the next few days. You have a passport, don't you? Can you give me some help?

Answer A I'll come shopping with you. You know, I love buying nice stuff! I have some ideas for gifts. Later, Susan

Question 2 I'm going to book my flight to Tokyo next week. Is it better to go to a travel agency, or do it online? Help!

Answer B Yeah, I spent a whole summer in Japan. I'll come over on Sunday and help you decide what to take. And I'll tell you all about Japan.
Tamara

Question 3 I'm going to buy gifts for my host family tomorrow. Do you want to come along? I need some ideas!

Answer C You can't take a taxi! We'll pick you up from the airport. It's no trouble at all. See you soon! Chieko

Question 4 Are you guys going to see me off at the airport? I'm not going to see you for three months, so I'd like you to come.

Answer D Sure, I'll help you with the application. It's very easy. Meet later today? Dan

Question 5 I'm going to pack my bags tomorrow, but I don't know what to take with me. You've been to Japan at this time of year. What clothes do I need to take?

Answer E I'll give our travel agent a call and check the prices. Then I'll check online. I'll let you know tomorrow.
XXXX Dan

Question 6 Dear Mr. & Mrs. Yoshioka, I'm going to take a taxi from the airport to your house. I think that will be easy for you.

Answer F Yes, we'll definitely come to the airport to say goodbye.
Dan, Tamara and Susan

Reading

1 Kelly is planning an exchange trip to Japan. Match her questions with her friends' answers.

1 _D_   4 ___
2 ___   5 ___
3 ___   6 ___

2 Read and listen to the e-mails. Circle the correct words.

1 Kelly's host family is going to send a taxi for her / meet her at the airport.
2 Kelly's friends are / aren't going to say goodbye at the airport.
3 Kelly has / doesn't have a passport.
4 Kelly hasn't decided / has decided what gifts to take to Japan.
5 One of Kelly's friends lives in Japan / has visited Japan.
6 One of Kelly's friends knows / is a travel agent.

Grammar

going to and *will*

Talking about plans and offers

1 Look at the chart.

Plan	Offer
I'm going to apply for my passport.	I'll help you.
I'm not going to see you for three months.	We'll come to the airport to say goodbye.

2 Read the sentences. Write P (for plan) or O (for offer).

1 "Is your math homework difficult? I'll help you."
   _O_

2 "I'm going to help David with his math homework tomorrow." ___

3 "I'm definitely going to go to the party on Saturday. See you there!" ___

4 "I forgot to tell David to cancel our reservations!" "I'll call him now." ___

5 "My CD player stopped working." "I'll fix it for you." ___

6 "How about going to a movie tonight?" "I can't. I'm going to visit my aunt." ___

3 Complete the plans and offers. Use the verbs in parentheses. Then match the plans and offers.

Plans

1 "I'_m going to take_ the six o'clock train." (take) _c_

2 "I _____ this dress!" (not wear) ___

3 "We _____ a rock band." (start) ___

4 "I _____ this bag. Its too heavy!" (not take) ___

5 "I _____ Grandpa next week." (visit) ___

Offers

a "I _'ll play_ the drums." (play)

b "I _____ with you. I'd like to see him." (come)

c "I _____ you a ride to the station." (give)

d "I _____ you carry it." (help)

e "I _____ you my red one." (lend)

4 Look at the pictures. Make offers to these people. Use the phrases from the box.

> call a taxi   clean it up   explain it to you
> help you find it   show you the way

1 _I'll show you the way_ .
2 _____ .
3 _____ .
4 _____ .
5 _____ .

Finished?
Page 105, Puzzle 3A

Over to you!

5 Make some plans. Use the ideas in the box. Can the class help you with your plans?

> go on a trip   buy some new clothes
> learn to ski   paint my room
> read more books

Student A: I'm going to go on a trip.
Student B: I'll help you pack.
Student C: I'll book your ticket for you.

3 Foreign exchange

Building the topic

Vocabulary

1 Match the pictures with the phrases below.

- ☑ be homesick for
- ☐ be rude
- ☐ make friends with
- ☐ get lost
- ☐ not get along with
- ☐ not fit in
- ☐ not understand

🎧 **Now listen and repeat.**

2 Kelly is worried about her trip to Japan. Look at the pictures and complete the sentences with the verbs from exercise 1.

1 I'm terrible with maps. I might _____get lost_____.

2 I don't speak much Japanese. I might _____ _____ anyone.

3 I don't know the Yoshioka family at all. I might _____ them.

4 I don't like to be away from my family for long. I might _____ my family.

5 I don't know their customs. I might _____ _____ by accident.

6 They look different from me and wear different types of clothes. I might _____.

7 I have a chance to meet lots of students, so I might _____ some fun people.

🎧 **Now listen and check.**

Grammar

might

Talking about future possibilities

1 Look at the chart.

Affirmative	Negative
I **might** get lost.	I **might not** fit in.

2 These people are sure about the future. You aren't sure. Change these certain predictions into uncertain predictions. Use *might* (*not*).

1   I'll win the race.

    You *might not win the race* .

2   We'll be late for dinner.

    You _____ .

3   He'll pass the test.

    He _____ .

4   The bus won't come on time.

    The bus _____ .

5   They'll call tonight.

    They _____ .

3 Complete the dialog. Use the words in parentheses.

Dan: I hear you're going to the U.S. on an exchange program. Are you going to visit New York?

Beth: (1)*I might not have time* (not have time). There are so many places to visit!

Dan: What about Los Angeles?

Beth: (2)_____ (go there). I hear it's really cool.

Dan: What about Austin, Texas? There's a lot of great music there.

Beth: Yes, (3)_____ (visit Austin). I'm going to stay in Houston, and it's not far away.

Dan: That's cool. What else are you going to do?

Beth: I'm not sure. I'd like to visit Mexico, but

    (4)_____

    (not have enough money).

    (5)_____

    (visit Sue) in Atlanta. I'd love to see her!

Dan: Cool!

4 Katie is going to go on a cruise. Write sentences with *might* or *might not* and the words in parentheses.

1   *She might not have the right clothes* .

    (have the right clothes)

2   _____ .

    _____ .

    (get bored)

3   _____

    _____ .

    (like the food)

4   _____

    _____ .

    (get lost on the ship)

5   _____

    _____ .

    (make some new friends)

6   _____

    _____ .

    (miss the ship)

Finished?
Page 105, Puzzle 3B

Over to you!

5 One student names a place, activity or event. The first student to make a good sentence with *might* / *might not* names the next thing.

Student A: Istanbul.

Student B: I might visit Istanbul this summer.

Student A: Good. Your turn.

Student B: Tattoo.

Student C: I might get a tattoo next year.

Living English

From Manila to Minnesota

An exchange student talks about her experiences and gives some valuable advice.

1 My name is Evelyn Garrido, and I'm from the Philippines. I've always wanted to be an exchange student, and when I was 16, I went to the U.S. My experience was amazing! I thought I knew a lot about the U.S., but there were a lot of things that surprised me too.

2 I stayed with a family in a small town in Minnesota, in the northern U.S. I just took a few long-sleeved shirts with me. I didn't take a warm coat. Big mistake! It was freezing. Take my advice – find out what clothes to take with you before you go.

3 My host family was wonderful, and most of the time I fit in with them and I didn't feel homesick. People in the U.S. are more informal. It's easy to talk to strangers, but it takes a long time to make friends.

4 People in Minnesota were interested in me because I was different. They wanted me to speak my language to them, and sometimes they asked me silly questions like, "Do you wear regular clothes at home?" or "Have you ever eaten ..." some gross thing they can think of. Be patient and understanding, and answer their questions.

5 My experience as an exchange student taught me a lot about other people and their culture, and I also learned a lot about myself. I feel more independent and I'm a stronger person now. I love traveling, and I think I might go to college in the U.S. I have my family and friends in the Philippines, and now I have friends and a second family in the U.S. too.

Reading 🎧

Before you read

1 Look at the photograph and the title. What do you think the article is about?

1 Evelyn's experience in Manila
2 Evelyn's experience in Minnesota

While you read

2 Look at the Reading skills box.

Reading skills

Paragraph topics

Each paragraph in a text has one main topic.

> Read the article once. Match the topics with the paragraphs. Write the number of the paragraph next to the topic.

the weather _2_   personal changes ___
introduction ___   relationships ___
cultural differences ___

After you read

3 Read the article again. Circle the correct answers.

1 Evelyn was 15 / 16 / 17 when she decided to become an exchange student.

2 The weather in Minnesota was cold / warm / sunny.

3 She felt like a stranger / a member of the family at her host family's home.

4 When people in your host country ask strange questions, you should refuse to answer / answer nicely.

5 Evelyn's experience in the U.S. taught her a lot about herself only / herself and other people.

Listening 🎧

1 Listen to the conversation once. What two things is Alicia possibly going to do?

2 Listen to the conversation again. Circle T (True) or F (False).

1 Alicia is definitely going to go to the art gallery.
T / (F)
2 People normally have to pay more to see the French art exhibition.
T / F
3 As Bob's guest, Alicia won't have to pay for a ticket to see the exhibition.
T / F
4 Alicia is going to go to a party right after she visits the art gallery.
T / F
5 Bob offers to go shopping with Alicia.
T / F
6 Bob plans to show Alicia a store where he buys his clothes.
T / F

Speaking 🎧

1 Listen and read.

2 Look at the Pronunciation box. Listen to the examples.

Pronunciation

Long and short vowels: /iː/ and /i/

/iː/ and /i/ are different sounds. /iː/ is a long sound. /i/ is a short sound.

/iː/	/i/
see	visit

Listen again and repeat.

3 Listen to the sounds of the vowels in red. Put the words into the correct column.

big   clean   important   meet   pizza
read   sleeve   this

/iː/	/i/
meet	this

4 Practice the dialog with your partner.

5 Change the words in blue. Write a new dialog. Now practice the dialog in class.

Review 3

Vocabulary
Travel expressions

1 **Fill in the blanks with the expressions below.**

> apply for a passport   book a flight   pick us up
> packed his bags   take a taxi   see me off

1 My friends are going to _see me off_ at the airport.

2 Joaquin's clothes are all over his room. He hasn't _____ yet.

3 My travel agent is going to _____ to London for me.

4 They aren't going to take the train to the airport. They're going to _____.

5 My friends are going to _____ in their car at the airport.

6 Dan forgot to _____. He can't go to France.

Living overseas

2 **Match the sentences 1–6 with the phrases a–f.**

1 I like the same fashion and music.
2 Where am I?
3 We never argue.
4 You're stupid!
5 What does this mean?
6 I'm not happy. I want to see my mom!

a be homesick
b be rude
c not understand
d fit in
e get along
f get lost

Grammar
going to

1 **Fill in the blanks with the *going to* form of the verbs in parentheses.**

1 I _'m going to study_ art in New York City. (study)

2 Karl _____ to Alaska New York. (go)

3 We _____ two months in Europe this summer. (spend)

4 Cara _____ in the race. (not run)

5 Sam and Paul _____ their grandparents today. (not visit)

will

2 **Make offers with *will* and the words below.**

> carry   explain   fix   make   translate

1 I _'ll fix_____ your computer for you.

2 I _____ the exercise for you.

3 I _____ a sandwich for you.

4 I _____ the Spanish for you.

5 I _____ that heavy bag for you.

might

3 **Look at the pictures. Fill in the blanks with *might* or *might not* and the verbs below.**

> catch   fall   have   lose

1 He _might not_ _catch_ the train.

2 Be careful! You _____ _____!

3 She _____ _____enough money.

4 The Blues _____ _____ the match.

Grammar: past progressive and simple past; past progressive and simple past (*when*)
Vocabulary: sleeping and dreaming; making things

Introducing the topic

Vocabulary

1 Match the pictures with the words below.

- [3] daydream
- [ ] have nightmares
- [ ] fall asleep
- [ ] wake up
- [ ] dream
- [ ] yawn

🎧 Now listen and repeat.

Recycling

2 How do you feel when you have a daydream? How do you feel when you have a nightmare? Write the words below in one of the columns.

| bored | creative | disappointed | embarrassed |
| excited | happy | nervous | scared |

Daydream	Nightmare
bored	disappointed

Exploring the topic

CREATIVE DREAMS

Nice tune

A Paul McCartney was a singer-songwriter in the famous pop group The Beatles. In May 1965, he was filming a movie in London. One night, he was sleeping at his house, and he had a dream. In the dream, he heard some beautiful music. When he woke up, he sat down at the piano and tried to play the music from his dream. He worked on the piano for hours and finally wrote *Yesterday*, the most popular song of the 20th Century.

Eureka!

B Elias Howe was an inventor. He wanted to invent a machine to make clothes. One day, he went to sleep and had a dream. In his dream, he was a prisoner and some men were dancing around him with spears. The spears had sharp points with holes in them. Suddenly, he woke up. The next morning, he was working again on the machine, and he had an idea. He put a hole at the end of the needle, and Eureka! – the machine worked.

Why not?

C Madame C.J. Walker was a poor African-American woman. She had a terrible problem. She was losing her hair. She tried different hair products, but nothing worked. One day, she had a dream. A man was telling her that there was a cure for her problem in Africa. Then, she woke up. She decided to experiment with different mixtures from Africa. One of the mixtures worked. Madame Walker began to sell her hair products. She became the first female Afican-American self-made millionaire.

Reading

1 Match the paragraphs A–C with the inventions below.

1 A needle for sewing machines *B*

2 A hair product ___

3 A famous pop song ___

2 🎧 Read and listen to the text. Circle T (True) or F (False).

1 Paul McCartney was staying in L.A. T /Ⓕ
2 He remembered the music from his dream. T / F
3 Elias Howe wasn't interested in the men's spears. T / F
4 He invented a new spear. T / F
5 Madame C.J. Walker's hair was falling out. T / F
6 She went to Africa to find a solution to her problem. T / F

Grammar
Past progressive and simple past

Describing scenes and sequences of events in the past

1 Look at the chart.

Describing the scene – past progressive	
Affirmative	Negative
He **was sleeping**.	He **wasn't working**.
They **were dancing**.	They **weren't singing**.

Sequence of events – simple past
He **fell** asleep. He **heard** some music. He **wrote** "Yesterday".

2 Fill in the blanks with the past progressive form of the verbs in parentheses.

1 I _____was playing_____ volleyball on a nice Caribbean beach. (play)

2 My friends _____ fun. (have)

3 My brother _____ the big waves. (surf)

4 You _____ about the weekend. (think)

5 She _____ to her boyfriend. (talk)

6 We _____ in a coffee house in New York. (sit)

3 Complete this dream with the verbs in parentheses. Use the past progressive affirmative or negative.

I was on a skiing vacation with a group of friends. It was my first skiing trip. We (1) _were having_ (have) a lesson with a ski instructor, and I (2) _____ (feel) very nervous. The instructor (3) _____ (teach) our group how to stop. My friends (4) _____ _____ (listen), but I (5) _____ (not pay) attention to the instructor. I (6) _____ (watch) another skier. He (7) _____ (ski) down the mountain really fast in my direction, and he was getting closer and closer …

4 Fill in the blanks with the verbs below. Use the simple past affirmative or negative.

crash	not fall	hit	not know	ski	stand

The man (1) ___crashed___ into me, but I (2) _____. I started moving down the mountain really fast on my skis. I was scared. I (3) _____ how to stop. Then the instructor (4) _____ past me very quickly. He turned and (5) _____ in front of me. I (6) _____ him and we both fell over.

Finished?
Page 107, Puzzle 4A

Over to you!

5 Describe a dream you remember well because it was scary, useful or funny.

Where were you? I was in a big house.

Who was with you? There were a lot of other people.

What were the other people doing? They were talking and having fun.

What were you doing? I was looking for an exit.

Compare your dreams in class.

4 Creative minds

Building the topic

DISCOVERED BY CHANCE

1 One day, a Swiss inventor, George de Mestral, was walking his dog in the mountains when the dog got covered with sticky seeds. Back home, he was removing the sticky seeds when he thought, "Why are they difficult to remove?" He then took two pieces of fabric and stuck some of the seeds on them. He pressed the two pieces together and they stuck, but you could also separate them.

2 It was a winter night. Eleven-year-old Frank Epperson was stirring a soda drink outside his house when it became very cold. He added some fruit flavors to it and he left his drink outside and went to bed. Frank was sleeping when the temperature fell below freezing. The drink froze with the stirring stick in it. In the morning, Frank was coming out of his house when he saw his drink. Frank showed his family the frozen soda. Many years later he invented a machine to make the frozen drink and sold it.

3 Art Fry was trying to find a good bookmark for his church songbook. His bookmarks always fell out. One day, he was singing at church when he suddenly had an idea. Fry used some weak adhesive. He put it on one of his bookmarks. The bookmark stuck to the page. Then he removed it, and the page didn't tear.

Vocabulary

1 Match the pictures with the words below.

☐5☐ add ☐ freeze ☐ press ☐ remove
☐ stir ☐ stick ☐ tear ☐ separate

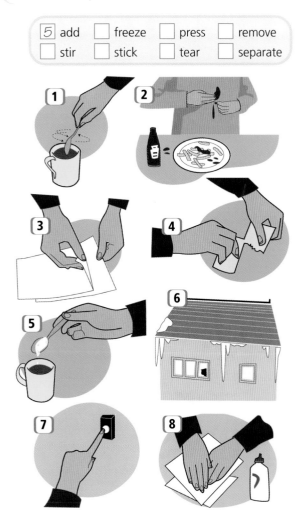

2 🎧 Read and listen to the text. Write the inventions next to the sentences.

Post-it note (1974)   Popsicle (1905)
Velcro (1948)

1 His friend's adhesive didn't damage paper.
   Post-it note

2 He left his drink outside in the cold one night.
   _____

3 His dog had lots of sticky seeds on him.
   _____

4 He put fruit flavors in the frozen drink.
   _____

5 The bookmarks stayed on the pages of a book. _____

6 He joined two pieces of fabric together.
   _____

🎧 **Now listen and repeat.**

36

Grammar

Past progressive and simple past (*when*)

Talking about an action in progress in the past when another action happened

1 Look at the chart.

Past progressive +	*when*	+ simple past
He **was walking** his dog		it **got covered** with sticky seeds.
He **was stirring** a drink	**when**	it **became** very cold.
He **was singing** at church		he suddenly **had** an idea.

2 Match the sentences 1–5 with the endings A–E.

1   He was stirring his drink *A*
2   I was opening the door ___

3   She was getting out of a car ___
4   He was ironing his pants ___

5   We were putting a book on a shelf ___

A   when his glass broke.
B   when a dictionary fell on my head.
C   when he burned them.
D   when the key got stuck in the lock.
E   when she tore her new dress.

3 Fill in the blanks with *when* and the simple past of the words in parentheses.

1   They were watching TV *when the door opened* . (door open)

2   They were sitting in a park _____ _____ on them. (dog / jump)

3   He was going upstairs _____. (fall)

4   He was having his dinner _____ _____ some wine on the table. (spill)

5   I was having a shower _____ _____. (telephone / ring)

6   We were sleeping _____ _____ a loud noise. (hear)

4 Fill in the blanks. Use the past progressive first, and then the past simple.

1   I *was going* (go) to the shop when I _____ (lose) my wallet.

2   Tom _____ (make) breakfast when he _____ (cut) his finger.

3   Dean and Tracey _____ (walk) to school when they _____ (see) an accident.

4   We _____ (play) soccer in the park when it _____ (start) to rain.

5   Judy _____ (watch) a movie when her friend _____ (call) on her cellphone.

6   My mom _____ (go) to bed when I _____ (arrive) home.

Finished?
Page 107, Puzzle 4B

Over to you!

5   Write four sentences. Can the class guess what happened to you?

Student A: I was dancing with Paul when …
Student B: The music stopped.
Student A: No.
Student B: Your parents came home.
Student A: Yes!

Living English

RECURRING DREAMS

Recurring dreams are dreams that you have many times, for example, dreams like running away or falling. What do they mean?

1 _____

I was looking for my classroom at school. I had an important test. I looked into a lot of rooms, and I finally found the right one. I was completely unprepared for the test and I felt sick. The test was too difficult. I was out of breath. I woke up.

Tessa, Canada

Meaning: You probably have some difficult situations in your life and you're worried.

2 _____

Someone was running after me at my old school. The school was very dark and empty. I was running very slowly. My feet were very heavy, and they were sticking to the floor. I was scared. The man was coming nearer and nearer. I didn't see his face. I tried to move and shout for help. Then I woke up.

Kosuke, Japan

Meaning: The man represents the things you feel scared about.

3 _____

I was on vacation with some friends. We were walking through a forest when I fell into a hole in the ground. The hole was dark and narrow. I shouted for help, but my friends didn't hear me. They were laughing and they were walking away from me. I held on to a tree, but it broke. I was falling faster and faster. When I was near the bottom of the hole, I woke up.

Ruben, Belgium

Meaning: You probably feel insecure, and you don't have any support or help.

4 _____

I was coming back from my gym class, when my mom said: "Hurry! You're getting married. It's time to go". I was sweaty and tired. I arrived at the wedding with my gym clothes on. I was late. Everybody was waiting for me and looking at me. I was in a panic. Then I woke up.

Julia, Mexico

Meaning: You probably don't feel very confident.

Reading 🎧

Before you read

1 What is a recurring dream? Do you have recurring dreams?

While you read

2 Look at the Reading skills box.

Reading skills

Getting the general idea

To get the general idea of a text, first read quickly and don't stop for difficult words.

Titles and pictures can help.

Now read the text. Write the headings in the correct place.

> being chased   being late and embarrassed
> falling   poor performance

After you read

3 Read the text again. Circle the correct option.

1 Kosuke was running away in her dream because she felt embarrassed / scared in real life.

2 Ruben was falling fast in his dream because he felt insecure / worried.

3 Julia arrived dirty and late in her dream because she was embarrassed / wasn't confident.

4 Tessa didn't perform well because she didn't have any help / had difficult situations in her life.

Listening 🎧

1 Listen to the story. Put the pictures in the correct order.

2 Listen again. Write the correct name (Mike or Rocky) in the blanks.

1 The girl was walking with her brother and her dog ___Rocky___.

2 At the beginning of the story, _____ was sitting in the stroller because he was tired.

3 _____ didn't like walking and refused to move.

4 The girl carried _____ back home.

5 When they got home, _____ was sitting in the stroller.

6 _____ wasn't tired when he got home.

Speaking 🎧

1 Listen and read.

What was your class doing when the fire alarm went off?

We were doing experiments in the lab.

Were you going to the club when you got lost?

No, I wasn't. I was going to your house.

2 Look at the Pronunciation box. Listen to the examples.

> **Pronunciation**
>
> Weak and strong forms of *was* and *were*
>
> **In the affirmative, we pronounce *was* as /wez/ and *were* as /we/.**
>
> **Weak forms**
>
> I was listening to music. We were singing.
>
> **In short answers to questions, we pronounce *was* as /wʌz/ and *were* as /wer/.**
>
> **Strong forms**
>
> Yes, he was. Yes, they were.

Listen again and repeat.

3 Listen to the sentences. <u>Underline</u> the weak forms and ⊙circle the strong forms.

1 I <u>was</u> playing soccer.
2 Yes, I was.
3 Yes, we were.
4 They were making dinner.

Now listen and repeat.

4 Practice the dialog with your partner.

5 Change the words in blue. Write a new dialog. Now practice the dialog in class.

Review 4

Vocabulary
Sleeping and dreaming

1 Correct the sentences. Use the words below.

> daydream   dream   falls asleep   nightmare
> wake up

dream
1   I often ~~yawn~~ about school and my friends there.

2   Do you <u>have nightmares</u> when you're bored?

3   My dad is very tired in the evenings, and he often <u>wakes up</u> on the sofa in front of the TV.

4   I usually <u>fall asleep</u> at seven o'clock every morning.

5   I had a <u>daydream</u> last night. I was in a dark forest and a lion was running after me.

Making things

2 Find eight verbs.

Grammar
Past progressive

1 Fill in the blanks in the stories with the words below. Use the past progressive.

> drink   get on   listen   open   read   travel
> wait   walk

A   I (1) *was traveling* to school by bus. There was a cool guy on the bus called Clive. He (2) _____
_____ to his MP3 player.
I (3) _____ to the front of the bus, but then the bus suddenly started to move, and …

B   I was sitting on the bus next to the coolest girl in school. She (4) _____ a magazine.
I (5) _____ some soda, then …

C   I (6) _____ for my bus. It arrived. The door (7) _____ . I (8) _____ the bus, then …

Simple past

2 Complete the stories with the words below. Use the simple past.

> close   fall   get stuck   hit   spill   stop

A   I _*fell*_ and _____ the boy in his face.

B   The bus _____ and I _____ soda on the girl's dress.

C   The door _____ and I _____ in the door.

Past progressive and simple past (*when*)

3 Fill in the blanks. Use the past progressive and the simple past of the words in parentheses.

1   Mary _*was stirring*_ (stir) her coffee when she _*spilled*_ some on her favorite dress.

2   Emma _____ (ask) her teacher a question when she _____ (forget) her name!

3   Shania _____ (dance) in a club when she _____ (fall) on the floor.

4   Gary _____ (paint) the door when the door _____ (close) on his thumb.

Reading

1 Read the story and answer the questions.

1   Who was Einstein?
2   What was he doing in the U.S.A.?
3   What was special about his chauffeur Harry?
4   What happened after Harry's lecture?
5   What did Harry do?

A TRUE STORY

The Nobel Prize scientist Albert Einstein was giving talks on his theory of relativity in the U.S.A. His chauffeur Harry always came to his talks. Harry was clever and admired Einstein. He could repeat the theory of relativity without making a mistake.

One day, Einstein had an idea. He invited Harry to be "Einstein" for one lecture. Harry happily said yes, and gave a perfect talk in front of a lot of people. Einstein sat at the back of the room. He was pretending to be the chauffeur. After the talk, Harry was walking to the car when a man stopped him and asked him a very difficult question. Harry replied, "The answer to this question is so simple that I'm going to ask my chauffeur".

5 Performing

Grammar: comparative adjectives / (*not*) *as ... as*; superlative adjectives
Vocabulary: describing sports; music

Introducing the topic

1 You can have an accident.
dangerous

2 It's really difficult.
_____

3 I want to win!
_____

4 You can get hurt.
_____

5 I can burn a lot of calories.
_____

6 We go at high speeds.
_____

Vocabulary

1 Label the sports with the adjectives below.

> competitive   dangerous   energetic   fast
> hard   rough

🎧 Now listen and repeat.

Recycling

2 Name the activities in the pictures in exercise 1.

1   *horseback riding*   4 _____
2 _____   5 _____
3 _____   6 _____

41

Exploring the topic

RUGBY, SOCCER OR FOOTBALL?

Todd, 17, New Zealand
Rugby is more exciting than football or soccer. I play rugby after school and I love it! We play on a bigger field than football fields, and we have more players than football. Rugby is as competitive as football, but it isn't as rough. You need protective clothing to play football. Rugby is more interesting than soccer too. Soccer is OK when you watch teams like Real Madrid or Manchester United, but it's usually slower and more boring than rugby or football.

Alex, 19, New York
Do you really think rugby is more exciting than football? You're wrong! Rugby isn't as energetic as football, but it's definitely more dangerous than football. Rugby players get seriously injured during games. I love football! It's faster and more exciting than rugby. I agree with you about soccer. I don't like soccer. I can't understand why people are crazy about it. Anyway, football is harder than rugby or soccer.

Manuela, 16, Brazil
Sorry to disagree guys. Soccer is much more fun, and the rules are easier than rugby and football. I don't understand the rules of those sports. It's a nicer game than rugby and football too because it isn't as rough. However, I think it's as hard as rugby and football, and it's more popular than those sports. I love the World Cup with teams and supporters from all around the world. Soccer isn't as expensive, and you don't need protective clothing. You can play soccer anywhere: in a park, on the street, and on the beach. The only thing you need is a ball and some friends.

Reading

1 Read the text. What are the three young people discussing?

a the history of sports
b their favorite sports
c why they don't play sports

2 🎧 Read and listen to the text. Circle T (True) or F (False). Correct the false sentences.

1 Manuela can understand the rules of soccer. T / F
2 Todd thinks rugby is hard and exciting. T / F
3 Alex thinks rugby isn't very dangerous. T / F
4 Todd thinks soccer can be slow and boring sometimes. T / F
5 Manuela thinks rugby and football aren't rough games. T / F
6 Manuela thinks soccer is very popular. T / F
7 Alex thinks football is more energetic than rugby. T / F

Grammar
Comparative adjectives
Talking about differences

1 Look at the chart.

Short comparative adjectives			
Soccer is	slow**er**	**than**	rugby.
Soccer rules are	eas**ier**	**than**	rugby rules.
We play rugby in a	big**ger** field	**than**	football.
Soccer is	nice**r**	**than**	football.

Long comparative adjectives			
Rugby is	**more** exciting	**than**	football.
Rugby and football are	**more** dangerous	**than**	soccer.

Take note!
Spelling rules

Short adjectives
1 Add -er or -r
fast → faster
nice → nicer
2 y + -ier
easy → easier
3 Double the consonant + -er
big → bigger

Long adjectives
exciting → more exciting

Irregular:
good → better
bad → worse

2 Fill in the blanks with the correct comparative form of the adjectives in parentheses.
1 Ice hockey is _____ *faster than* _____ field hockey. (fast)
2 I think basketball is _____ tennis. (energetic)
3 I think baseball is _____ golf. (hard)
4 Tennis is _____ table tennis. (exciting)
5 Rugby players are _____ horse riders. (big)
6 The hockey ball is _____ the tennis ball. (heavy)
7 Do you think European stadiums are _____ American stadiums? (good)
8 A basketball is _____ a golf ball. (large)

(not) as ... as
Talking about similarities and differences

3 Look at the chart.

(not) as ... as	Meaning
Rugby is **as competitive as** football.	Rugby and football are competitive.
Rugby is **not as rough as** football.	Football is rougher than rugby.

4 Make sentences using *as ... as.*
1 Surfing is exciting. Windsurfing is exciting.
Surfing is as exciting as windsurfing .
2 Bungee jumping is dangerous. Rock climbing is dangerous. _____
3 Climbing equipment is heavy. Skiing equipment is heavy. _____
4 Skating is difficult. Snowboarding is difficult. _____
5 Rafting is hard. Kayaking is hard. _____

5 Make sentences using *not as ... as.*
1 (fast) skating – / snowboarding +
Skating isn't as fast as snowboarding .
2 (energetic) golf – / tennis +
3 (dangerous) soccer – / rugby +
4 (rough) baseball – / ice hockey +
5 (expensive) rafting – / sailing +

Finished?
Page 107, Puzzle 5A

Over to you!
6 **Compare two popular sports in your country. Compare your ideas in class.**
Student A: Soccer is faster and more competitive than volleyball.
Student B: I like volleyball. It isn't as fast as soccer, but it's more energetic.

Building the topic

Musical records

1 Glastonbury is one of the most popular music festivals in the world. About 150,000 people go to the festival to see their favorite bands.

2 The performance of Organ2 (or ASLSP) is the slowest concert in the world. It began in 2001 and it's going to finish in 2639! The orchestra plays in an empty church in Germany. (The abbreviation ASLSP means As Slow As Possible.)

3 The oldest song in the world is a Syrian religious song. It's from about 1400 B.C.

4 The stalacpipe organ lies deep underground in the Luray Caverns in Virginia, U.S.A. It's the largest musical instrument in the world, and it uses stalactites to make its sound.

5 Ricky Brown is the fastest rapper in the world. In 2005, in Washington, U.S.A., he rapped 723 syllables in 41.27 seconds on his track NoClue.

Glastonbury Festival, U.K.

Buchardi church organ, Halberstadt, Germany

Stalacpipe organ, Luray Caverns, Virginia, U.S.A.

Vocabulary

1 Fill in the blanks with the words below.

> album   band   festival   instruments   orchestra
> tracks

1 Can you play any musical _instruments_, like the piano or the guitar?

2 The Creamfields Virtual Electronic Music _____ is at the end of August every year.

3 A symphony _____ has over eighty musicians. They play instruments like the violin, the cello, and the piano.

4 Muse is a very popular British _____.

5 Fionna Apple is an American singer. Her _____ title is very long. It has 90 words!

6 Did you know there can be 99 _____ on a CD?

🎧 **Now listen and repeat.**

2 🎧 **Read and listen to the text. Circle T (True) or F (False). Then correct the false sentences.**

1 Glastonbury is a popular music festival. Ⓣ/ F

2 The first song was a national anthem. T / F

3 The biggest instrument is in a church in Germany. T / F

4 Organ2 is a long music piece. T / F

5 Ricky Brown played a very slow rap in 2005. T / F

Grammar

Superlative adjectives

Talking about unique things

1 **Look at the chart.**

> **Superlative adjectives**
>
> Ricky Brown is **the** fast**est** rapper in the world.
>
> Glastonbury is one of **the most** popular festivals in the U.K.

> ## Take note!
>
> **Spelling rules**
>
> | **Short adjectives** | **Long adjectives** |
> |---|---|
> | **1** Add -*est* or -*st* | interesting → the most interesting |
> | old → the oldest | |
> | **2** ~~y~~ + -*iest* | **Irregular** |
> | easy → the easiest | good → the best |
> | **3** Double the consonant + -*est* | bad → the worst |
> | big → the biggest | |

2 **Circle the correct form of the superlative.**

1 Qatar has (the biggest) / the most big sports dome in the world. It's 290,000 square meters.
2 Kiel Week is the largest / the most large sailing event in the world. There are more than 2,000 boats.
3 Glasgow in Scotland has the tallest / the most tall movie theater in the world.
5 The city of Virginia has the goodest / the best skate park in the USA.
6 Cannes in France holds one of the popularest / the most popular film festivals in the world.

3 **Fill in the blanks in the quiz. Do you know the answers?**

1 The *biggest* (big) selling album in the world in 2005 was:
  a American Idiot (Green Day)   b X&Y (Coldplay)
2 Ghost, _____ (long) music video in 1996, lasted 35 minutes. It was by:
  a Madonna   b Michael Jackson
3 _____ (successful) virtual band in 2001 was:
  a Juju Eyeballs   b Gorillaz
4 _____ (expensive) video in 1995 cost seven million dollars. It was:
  a Scream (Michael Jackson)   b Victory (Puff Daddy)
5 _____ (young) artist to have a U.S. Number 1 was thirteen (1963). He was:
  a John Lennon   b Stevie Wonder

4 **Fill in the blanks with the comparative or superlative form.**

1 He's ___the coolest___ rap artist on stage. (cool)
  He's _cooler than_ than Dr Dre! (cool)
2 Your guitar is _____ my guitar. (expensive) It's _____ guitar in the band. (expensive)
3 A: I think Mariah Carey is _____ Shania Twain. (good)
  B: You're kidding me. Shania Twain is _____ _____ singer in the world. (good)
4 The Reading Festival is _____ three-day rock festival in the U.K. (large)
5 The piano is _____ instrument to play. (easy) It's _____ the guitar. (easy)

> **Finished?**
> Page 107, Puzzle 5B

> ## Over to you!
>
> **5** **In your opinion:**
> 1 Which is the best band in the world?
> 2 Who's the best singer?
> 3 Which is the best album/song?
> 4 What's the best dance music?
> I think Sugababes is the best band in the world.
>
> **Ask and answer in class.**

Living English

Try something different!

The Silent Disco

This is the biggest and the quietest disco in the world. Thousands of people meet up on streets with their MP3 players. They choose the music they like, play the music, and dance. It looks really strange. The street is silent, but it's full of people dancing to different styles of music: rap, pop, electronic, and so on. There are silent discos in the Netherlands, the U.K. and Canada. This activity isn't suitable for shy people!

Bossaball

The idea is to play different sports and listen to Latin music at the same time. You can see people playing volleyball or soccer to the rhythm of salsa music. It's a new sport from Belgium. It's safer than a regular game of volleyball or soccer, because it has a soft field. It's good exercise and it's a lot of fun.

Pillow Fight Club

Thousands of people meet up in a public place in the center of their city. They carry pillows in a plastic bag. When the event starts, they take out their pillows and start to fight. The event can continue for minutes or hours! It's as exciting as pillow fights in your bedroom, but it's much, much bigger. Pillow fights take place in countries all around the world.

Reading 🎧

Before you read

1 Look at the photos. What are the people doing?

While you read

2 Read the text. Match the words to the activities.

1 MP3 players + streets + people _C_

2 street + pillows + people ___

3 volleyball + trampoline + salsa ___

A a sport
B an event
C an outside dance club

After you read

3 Read the text again. Circle T (True) or F (False).

1 All the people in the street can hear the music. (T)/ F

2 At a silent disco, people listen to the same music. T / F

3 Bossaball is a dangerous sport. T / F

4 Bossaball is a good sport because you listen to music and play at the same time. T / F

5 The Pillow Fight Club is a street event. People carry a pillow and sleep in the street. T / F

6 A pillow fight can be long or short. T / F

Writing

1 Look at the Writing skills box.

Writing skills

Expressing opinions

When you want to give your opinion, write *I think*, *I don't think*, or *In my opinion*, at the beginning of a sentence.

I think electronic music is the best dance music.

I don't think it's the best dance music. It's boring.

In my opinion, hip hop is the best dance music.

2 Now read the text. Circle examples of *I think*, *I don't think*, and *In my opinion*.

Pop or rap?

Hi. I'm Jess. I like pop music. I think it's quieter than rap music. In my opinion, the words in pop songs are clearer than the words in rap songs. They're easier to understand and I can sing the songs with my friends. Rap songs are more negative and I can't remember the words.
I think rap is fun. It's more energetic than pop music. I don't think it's aggressive. The videos are better than pop videos. Pop singers are good-looking, but rappers look cooler than pop stars, and the dancers are amazing.

3 Fill in the chart with Jess's opinion about pop and rap.

POP	
music	*quieter*
words	
singers	
RAP	
music	
words	
singers	

4 Now make notes about two music styles.

5 Write a comparison of the music styles in exercise 4. Use the text and your notes to help you.

Speaking

1 Listen and read.

2 Look at the Pronunciation box. Listen to the examples.

Pronunciation

Word stress

It is important to know where the stress goes in words with three syllables.

1 <u>fun</u>nier   2 ex<u>ci</u>ting

Listen again and repeat.

3 Listen and underline the stress in these words.

agg<u>res</u>sive   arrogant   dangerous   expensive
instrument   orchestra

Listen again and repeat.

4 Practice the dialog with your partner.

5 Change the words in blue. Write a new dialog. Now practice the dialog in class.

Review 5

Vocabulary

Describing sports

1 Unscramble the two adjectives. Cross out the one which is not true.

1 A motorbike is safafest.
   ___fast___ ~~safe~~

2 Chess is enehargerdtic.
   _____ _____

3 Computer games are bexociringting.
   _____ _____

4 Motor racing is danrougeghrous.
   _____ _____

5 Soccer is excompenpetisivetive.
   _____ _____

Music

2 Fill in the missing letters in these music words.

1 _b_ _a_ _n_ _d_   4 i _ _ _ _ _ u _ e _ _
2 a _ _ u _   5 o _ _ _ _ e _ _ _ _ a
3 _ _ a _ _   6 _ e _ _ i _ a _

Grammar

Comparative adjectives; as ... as

1 Complete Jess's opinion with the comparative form of the words in parentheses, or as ... as.

> **Sports at school**
>
> We can play two sports at school: netball (women's basketball) and field hockey.
> I play field hockey every Friday. I think it's
> (1) _more exciting than_ (exciting) netball.
> Netball is OK. It's probably (2) _____
> (easy) hockey. It isn't (3) _____
> (fast) hockey, and it isn't (4) _____
> (hard) hockey.
> In my opinion, netball is (5) _____
> (difficult) hockey. Netball players are (6) _____
> _____(fit) hockey players because they need
> to jump high to score a goal. People say netball
> isn't (7) _____ (rough) hockey.
> I don't agree. Any team sport can be rough.

Superlative adjectives

2 Fill in the blanks with the adjectives below in their superlative forms.

(colorful   dangerous   dirty   early   late   noisy)

1 The Kite Festival starts in March. It's _the_
   earliest festival of the year.

2 It's _____ festival. There are
   thousands of kites in different shapes and colors.

3 The Tomatina is _____ festival. The
   streets are full of tomatoes after the tomato fight.

4 It's _____ festival.
   People wear glasses to protect their eyes.

5 The Congaline has _____
   finishing time. It ends at 11 p.m.

6 It's probably _____ festival,
   with thousands of people singing and dancing.

Study skills

Using word lists

Word lists are useful when you're speaking or writing assignments in class. They're also useful to check your spelling when you're doing your homework.

1 Read the word list for Unit 5 on page 119 and choose some words to describe sports.
   competitive _____ _____

Verb lists are useful to find the past and perfect forms of irregular verbs.

2 Choose three verbs from the verb list on page 118. Write the verbs and the simple past forms below.

   _____ _____
   _____ _____
   _____ _____

Achievements

Grammar: present perfect (*for* / *since*); present perfect and simple past
Vocabulary: business; public activities

Introducing the topic

1 study something and find information about it

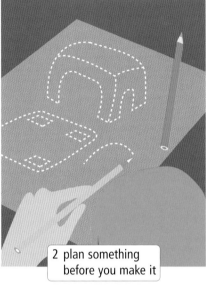

2 plan something before you make it

3 make something new

4 tell people about a product, for example in a magazine or on TV

5 give an object to a person for money

6 do well at something

Vocabulary

1 Match the pictures and their definitions with the words below.

- 4 advertise
- ☐ create
- ☐ design
- ☐ research
- ☐ sell
- ☐ be successful

🎧 Now listen and repeat.

Recycling

2 What are the personal nouns that come from the verbs?

advertise = _____*advertiser*_____

create = _____

design = _____

research = _____

sell = _____

Exploring the topic

A SWEET IDEA

Elise and Evan Macmillan's online candy company, Chocolate Farm, has been in business for more than nine years. They've had their own company since Elise was ten years old and Evan was thirteen!

Elise has made chocolate for more than fifteen years. Her grandmother taught her to make chocolate when she was three. Elise and Evan knew the chocolate was very good. They decided to sell their chocolate, and they were very successful.

Since 1998, Elise has researched different ways of making chocolate. She's created new products for the company, including chocolate-making kits for customers. They've received two important awards. They won an Ernst & Young Entrepreneur of the Year award in 1999, and they were one of the top youth food businesses in the U.S. in 2001.

A lot of people buy their products online. The website is a very important part of their business, and Evan is now an expert web-designer. He's designed websites since he was twelve.

More than forty people now work for Evan and Elise.

Reading

1 Read the article. What is the relationship between Evan and Elise? What does their company do?

2 🎧 Read and listen to the article. Fill in the blanks.

1 Elise and Evan Macmillan have had their own company for more than _nine years_ .

2 Elise has made chocolate since she was _____ .

3 Elise and Evan have sold their chocolate for _____ .

4 The company has produced many new products since _____ .

5 Evan has been a web-designer since he was _____ .

Grammar

Present perfect (*for* / *since*)

Talking about present activities that started in the past

1 Look at the chart.

Present perfect	for / since	
Chocolate Farm **has been** in business	**for**	nine years.
Elise and Evan **have had** their company	**since**	1998.

Take note!

We use *for* to talk about a period of time up to the present.

for twelve years, for three months, for two days, etc.

We use *since* to talk about activities that started at a point of time in the past.

since 1995, since last year, since she was ten ...

2 Circle *for* or *since*.

1 Janet has had her company since / (for) five years.
2 David has been a researcher since / for 1997.
3 People have eaten chocolate for / since over 2,000 years.
4 Their company has grown a lot since / for they started it in 2002.
5 Our local chocolate store has been open for / since 104 years.
6 Rob has had five jobs for / since he left school.

3 Write sentences with *since* and *for*.

1 Judith / live / Chicago / 2004

   Judith has lived in Chicago since 2004 .

2 She / be / a doctor / two years

_____

3 She / has / a dog / five years

_____

4 She / live / in her house / last summer

_____

5 She / do / karate / four months

_____

6 She / write / a blog / October

_____

Finished?
Page 107, Puzzle 6A

Over to you!

4 Think of three activities you do. Use *for* or *since* and tell the class how long you've done these activities. Can the class guess the activities?

Student A: My clue is: for six years.
Student B: Have you been a student at this school for six years?
Student A: No, I haven't.
Student B: Have you been on the hockey team for six years?
Student A: That's right! Your turn.

Building the topic

BONO: HELPING TO CHANGE THE WORLD

Bono is the lead singer in the band U2. The band has been very successful worldwide, and has sold more than a hundred million records. Bono is a great musician, but he's also done a lot more in his life.

ACHIEVEMENTS

Bono has helped organize some of the biggest charity concerts in the world, including Live Aid and Live 8. He's sung with a lot of other musicians, including opera singer Luciano Pavarotti, country singer Johnny Cash, and pop legend Paul McCartney. He's met politicians and leaders from around the world. He's campaigned for debt relief for the world's poorest countries. He's asked rich countries to cancel their debt. He's visited Africa many times to do humanitarian work.

BIOGRAPHY

Paul Hewson (Bono) was born in Dublin, Ireland, on May 10th, 1960.
He joined U2 in 1976, along with Larry Mullen Jr., Dave "The Edge" Evans, and Adam Clayton.
He married Ali, his high school girlfriend, on August 21st, 1982.
He appeared in the Live Aid concert in 1985. He raised money for hungry people in Ethiopia. He also appeared in Live 8 in 2005.
In 2002, he set up an organization called DATA to tell the world about Africa's problems, and how other countries can help.
In February 2006, Bono gave a speech. He asked governments to give more money to poorer countries.

Vocabulary

1 Write the words or phrases next to the definitions.

> appear   campaign   give a speech   organize
> raise money   set up

1 start a new group or organization __set up__

2 arrange or plan an event _____

3 collect money for charity _____

4 speak in front of the public about something important _____

5 be in a concert, in a show, or on TV _____

6 make people know about a bad situation in order to change it _____

🎧 **Now listen and repeat.**

2 🎧 **Read and listen to the text. Has Bono done these things? Write *Yes, he has* or *No, he hasn't*.**

1 Has he spoken in public with a world leader?
   Yes, he has .

2 Has he acted in movies? _____.

3 Has he sung with other musicians?
   _____.

4 Has he been a member of the government in Ireland? _____.

5 Has he sold lots of records? _____.

6 Has he lived in Africa? _____.

Grammar
Present perfect and simple past

Talking about personal achievements

1 Look at the chart.

Present Perfect	Simple past
Bono **has written** music for several movies. (we don't say when)	He **married** Ali in 1982. (we say when)

2 Read about Nicole Kidman. Circle the correct tense in each part of the sentences.

Nicole Kidman	
Achievements	**Facts**
30 movies	1983 – first movie
Worked with children's organizations	1994 – representative for UNICEF
Lived in Australia and the U.S.	1967 – born in Hawaii
Nominated for many awards	2003 – won Academy award for *The Hours*
Married twice	2006 – married Keith Urban

1 She has acted /(acted) in her first movie in 1983. She has made / made more than 30 movies.

2 Nicole has become / became a representative for the charity UNICEF in 1994. She has worked / worked with several organizations to help disadvantaged children.

3 She was born / has been born in Hawaii in 1967. She lived / has lived in Australia and the U.S.

4 The film industry has nominated / nominated Nicole for a lot of awards. She has won / won an Academy Award in 2003 for *The Hours*.

5 She has been / was married married twice. She has married / married country singer Keith Urban in 2006.

3 Complete the sentences. Use the verbs in parentheses in the simple past or present perfect.

1 Steve Jobs ___was___ born in San Francisco, California in 1955. (be)

2 He _____ Apple Computer Inc. with two other people in 1976. (set up)

3 He _____ other companies, including Pixar Animation Studios. (buy)

4 Pixar _____ its first feature film, *Toy Story*, in 1995. (make)

5 Pixar _____ many other popular movies, including *Monsters Inc.* and *Finding Nemo*. (produce)

4 Write sentences with the simple past or present perfect. Use the words in parentheses.

1 I / go to / two rock concerts / last year.
   I went to two rock concerts last year .

2 I / read / three *Harry Potter* books.
   _____.

3 I / see / two James Bond films / in September.
   _____.

4 I / travel to / two countries in Europe.
   _____.

5 I / visit / the U.S. / in 2004.
   _____.

Finished?
Page 107, Puzzle 6B

Over to you!

5 Write three things you've done in your life. Tell your partner the beginning of the sentence. Can the class guess the end of the sentence?

Student A: I've written ...
Student B: a song?
Student A: No.
Student B: a story?
Student A: Yes.
Student B: I've designed ...
Student C: a T-shirt?

Living English

Margaret Drew

Margaret Drew is 17 years old. She likes everything other regular teenagers like. The most important part of her life, however, is her school dance team. Margaret has been a member of the team since her first year at high school. Her coach says she's an inspiration to the rest of her team, and to teams around the state. People admire Margaret because she has Kniest syndrome. It means she's grown to only 106 cm tall. But she doesn't see this as a problem. When she was in middle school, she ran track races, and in seventh grade, she joined the volleyball team. Now, along with her dance team, she's hoping to win the State Championships.

Coach Caysie Duax has changed parts of the dance routine for Margaret, so that she can do them. However, Margaret's teammates often forget that she's shorter than them. She isn't discouraged by her height, and she takes part in all the activities. Margaret and the team believe in diversity. They believe that your height, weight, race, or gender aren't important. Caysie Duax wants Margaret to be on the team because she works hard, she loves dancing, and she gets along well with the rest of the team.

Reading 🎧

Before you read

1 Look at the photo. What is different about Margaret Drew?

While you read

2 Read the article once. Answer the questions.

1 What activity does Margaret do at school?
2 Why is Margaret shorter than the others on the team?

3 Look at the Reading skills box.

> ### Reading skills
> Meaning from context
>
> To understand new words, look at:
> • the complete sentence
> • the sentences before and after
> • the type of word (noun, verb, adjective, etc.)

Find these words in the article. Guess the meaning from the context and then circle the best choice.

1 inspiration: ⓐ a good example b a skilled athlete

2 admire: a respect   b worry about

3 syndrome: a a disease   b an ability

4 discouraged: a feeling confident
               b not feeling confident

5 diversity: a being different
               b being hard-working

After you read

4 Read the article again. Circle T (True) or F (False).

1 Margaret has different interests from other teenagers. T /Ⓕ

2 Margaret has sometimes wanted to stop her dance classes. T / F

3 Margaret doesn't take part in sports. T / F

4 Margaret does exactly the same movements as her teammates. T / F

5 Margaret's friends don't think about her height. T / F

6 According to the coach, Margaret belongs on the dance team. T / F

Listening

1 Listen to the conversation. What is David's favorite subject?

2 Listen to the conversation again. Put a ✓ next to the things David and Joanna have done. Put a ✗ next to the ones they haven't done.

	David	Joanna
be late with homework	✗	
stay up all night doing homework		
cheat on a test		
do the wrong homework		

Writing

1 Read the article. What does Armando do? What has he done to help others?

My name is Armando Abeya and I'm a singer. I started singing when I was ten years old. I made my first CD when I was sixteen, and it was very successful.

I've done a lot of things in my career. I've made twelve CDs and about fifteen music videos. I've appeared in many live concerts. I've written many songs, and I've written the music for a movie too. I've also won two awards: one for best Latin CD of the year, and one for best song.

I've visited a lot of schools in poor areas. I've set up a program to teach music in the schools.

2 Read the article again. Fill in the chart with Armando's information.

Name	*Armando Abeya*
Occupation	
Did in the past	
Have done	

3 Now imagine you are a successful business person, actor or singer. Make notes about yourself.

4 Write an article about yourself. Use the text and your notes to help you.

Review 6

Vocabulary

Business

1 Fill in the blanks with the words below.

> advertise   create   design   research
> sell   (be) successful

How to create a new product

(1) _Research_ the market. Find out what people want.

(2) _____ your product. Does it look good? (3) _____ in newspapers, magazines, and on TV.

(4) _____ a website for the product.

Now, (5) _____ your product and make some money.

Good luck! We hope you (6) _____ !

Public activities

2 Match the beginnings of the phrases 1–6 with the correct endings A–F.

1 campaign   A a company
2 set up   B a concert
3 raise money   C for debt relief
4 appear   D for charity
5 give a speech   E about your company
6 organize   F on TV

Grammar

Present perfect (*for* / *since*)

1 Fill in the blanks. Use the present perfect form of the verbs in parentheses, and *for* or *since*.

1 Jenny __'s been__ (be) a member of the dance team ____for____ three years.

2 My parents _____ (have) their own company _____ 2001.

3 John _____ (take) tennis lessons _____ more than a year.

4 I _____ (not see) Joe _____ six months.

5 I _____ (study) French _____ 2004.

Present perfect and simple past

2 Write about Matt Dark's career. Use the information below and the present perfect or the simple past.

> Matt Dark
> born: 1982, New York City
> number of movies: 12
> first movie: 1995
> awards received in career: 3
> Golden Globe award: 2004
> married: 2005

1 _Matt Dark was born in New York City in 1982_ .

2 _He's made 12 movies_ .

3 _____ .

4 _____ .

5 _____ .

6 _____ .

Reading

1 Answer the questions. Use one or two words.

1 What sport does Hannah Teeter do? _Snowboarding_

2 Who did Hannah want to be like?

3 What is Hannah like?

4 What part of Hannah's body did another snowboarder hurt?

5 What two things made it possible for Hannah to return to the competition after her injury?

Hannah Teeter Snowboard Champion

Hannah Teeter is a champion snowboarder. She's won several World Cup titles and she's also won an Olympic Gold Medal. Hannah is only 19 years old.

Hannah has four older brothers, and always wants to do the same things as they do. She started snowboarding and really liked it.

Hannah has competed in a lot of events since she entered competitive snowboarding. She's very strong and determined. At a World Cup event in Japan, another competitor fell on Hannah and injured Hannah's back. She soon returned to competing in the sport, thanks to hard work and training.

7 Do the right thing

Grammar: question tags; *make / let / be allowed*
Vocabulary: travel essentials; rules

Introducing the topic

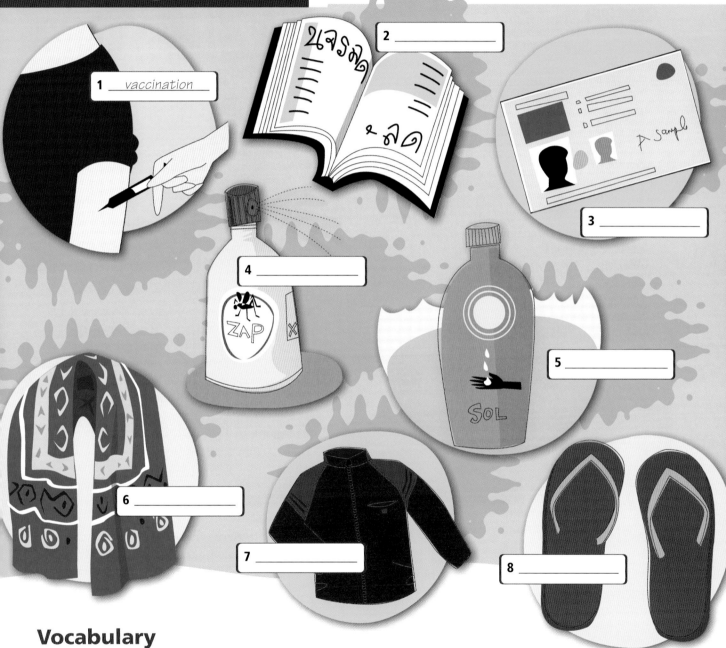

1 _vaccination_

2 _____

3 _____

4 _____

5 _____

6 _____

7 _____

8 _____

Vocabulary

1 Label the pictures with the verbs below.

> driver's license   flip-flops   insect spray
> phrase book   scarf   sunblock   vaccination
> wind jacket

🎧 Now listen and repeat.

Recycling

2 Write 3 words from exercise 1 for each verb below.

use: _insect spray_ _____ _____

wear : _____ _____ _____

57

Exploring the topic

Travel Advice

Traveling abroad? Do you need some advice about the places you're going to? Then e-mail us at Travel Advice.

Questions

1 I'm visiting Barbados on an exchange program. Most people speak English there, don't they?
Marcos, 16

2 I'm traveling to Bahrain in the Persian Gulf with a group of friends. There aren't any dress rules in Bahrain, are there?
Kate, 18

3 I'm backpacking in Thailand in November. It rains a lot at this time of the year, doesn't it?
Gareth, 17

4 A friend of mine is going to Zanzibar in Africa soon. She doesn't need a yellow fever vaccination, does she?
Renée, 17

5 My brother and I are traveling to Moscow. We're renting a car. We don't need an international driver's license, do we?
Ariel, 18

6 I'm planning to explore the outer islands of Vanuatu. The islanders are friendly to foreigners, aren't they? We're going there in October. It isn't cold then, is it?
Johnny, 19

Thailand

Bahrain

Answers

a No, she doesn't need a yellow fever vaccination, but malaria is a problem. She needs malaria tablets. It's her responsibility to take them every day. Tell your friend to sleep under a mosquito net.

b No, there's no formal code, but show respect for the culture of the people there. Don't wear shorts or short sleeveless dresses.

c The law is that you have to be 18 years old and carry an international driver's license. Remember to carry your passport and visa all the time.

d Yes, most people speak English, but they also speak Bajan. It's a mix of English and African languages.

e They certainly are and they're very helpful. It's warm in Vanuatu, but it can be very windy on the outer islands. You need to take the right clothes with you.

f Not really. The rainy season lasts from June to October, but it's hot and dry in November. Carry light clothes and sandals.

Zanzibar

Reading

1 **Read the text. Write the correct name next to the questions below.**

1 Can we use a normal driver's license? *Ariel*

2 Do I need to cover my head with a scarf?
   _____

3 Does my friend need a vaccination?
   _____

4 Do I need a phrase book? _____

5 Do we need wind jackets to keep warm?
   _____

6 Can I leave my sunblock at home?
   _____

2 **Read again and match the answers with the questions.**

1 _d_ 2 ___ 3 ___ 4 ___ 5 ___ 6 ___

🎧 **Now listen and check.**

Grammar
Question tags

Asking questions to check information

1 Look at the chart.

Question tags with *be*	
Affirmative statement + negative tag	Negative statement + affirmative tag
It's cold, **isn't** it? Islanders are friendly, **aren't they**?	It isn't cold, **is it**? **There aren't** any dress rules, **are there**?

Take note!

I'm late, **aren't I**?

2 Match the sentences about a trip to India with the correct question tag.

1 We're going to see the Taj Mahal, _E_

2 The River Ganges is in India, ___

3 Mount Everest isn't in India, ___

4 You aren't going to visit Sri Lanka, ___

5 The roads in India aren't busy, ___

6 I'm going to have a great trip, ___

A aren't they?   C aren't I?   E aren't we?
B is it?   D isn't it?   F are you?

3 Look at the chart.

Question tags with *do*	
Affirmative statement + negative tag	Negative statement + affirmative tag
It **rains** a lot, **doesn't it**?	She **doesn't need** a vaccine, **does she**?
Most people **speak** English, **don't they**?	We **don't need** a driver's license, **do we**?

4 Fill in the blanks. Use question tags with *do* in the affirmative or negative.

1 We have to go through passport control, _don't we_ ?

2 Students in Thailand wear uniforms, _____?

3 The people in Zanzibar don't collect coral reef, _____ ?

4 It doesn't rain a lot in August, _____ ?

5 "Da" means "Yes" in Russian, _____?

6 I don't need to take malaria tablets, _____?

5 Write the correct question tags. Use *be* or *do* in the affirmative or negative.

1 Vanuatu is in the Pacific Ocean, ___ _isn't it_ ?
   Yes, it is.

2 Canada's national game isn't baseball, _____?
   No, ice hockey is the country's national game.

3 Rap and hip hop aren't popular music styles, _____?
   Yes, they are.

4 The Arabic language doesn't read from left to right, _____?
   No, it reads from right to left and from top to bottom.

5 Tours to the Bulgarian caves don't leave early, _____?
   Yes, they do.

Finished?
Page 109, Puzzle 7A

Over to you!

6 Make five questions with tags to ask people in your class about their lives.

Student A: You're fifteen, aren't you?
Student B: No, I'm not. I'm sixteen.
Student A: Your dad works in an office, doesn't he?
Student B: Yes, he does.

Building the topic

RULES AND FREEDOM at School

- Summerhill school is a "free" school. It's different from a regular school. Students at this school are allowed to have a lot of freedom, and they learn to be responsible for their lives. Teachers don't make students go to classes. Students can decide to go to a class, or they can play on the school grounds. After a few weeks of freedom, most students go to classes because they want to learn.

- Summerhill is a boarding school. Students live at the school during the semester, and go home for the vacations. After classes, teachers let students do what they like with their own free time. They can play music, rehearse for a show, or read biology in a tree house, but they aren't allowed to play the drums at 4 a.m! They have to respect the other students, and they can't wake them up when they're asleep. Students aren't allowed to break this rule!

- Students are allowed to make important decisions. They have meetings with the staff and they decide on the school rules. The school lets students decide on rules for bedtimes, for using the kitchen, parking bikes, and picking up litter. The students have to obey these rules. They also discuss problems like bullying and being late for classes.

Do you have strict rules at your school? Would you like more freedom?

Vocabulary

1 Read the text. Then fill in the blanks with the words below.

> break (rules) bullying obey (rules) respect
> strict (be) responsible (for)

1 Our school is very ___strict___. We can't talk in class, and we aren't allowed to use cellphones.

2 I think _____ is terrible. It isn't right to frighten and hurt other people.

3 The rule is "No shouting". Tom is shouting. He's _____ing the rule.

4 The rule is "No eating". Sue isn't eating. She's _____ing the rule.

5 If you _____ people, you think about their needs and opinions.

6 It's your homework. You're _____ for doing it.

🎧 **Now listen and check.**

2 🎧 Read and listen to the text. Circle T (True) or F (False).

1 The school teaches students to be responsible. Ⓣ/ F

2 Students have to go to all their classes. T / F

3 The students live at the school all year. T / F

4 Students have to think about other students when they go to bed. T / F

5 Parents and teachers make the decisions at the school. T / F

Grammar

make / let / be allowed

Talking about obligation and permission

1 Look at the chart.

Obligation
The school **makes** children be responsible for their lives.
Teachers **don't make** students go to classes.

Permission
The school **lets** students decide on rules for bedtimes.
The school **doesn't let** students stay up after 10:30.
Students **are allowed** to have a lot of freedom.
They **aren't allowed** to play the drums at 4 a.m.

2 Match the speech bubbles 1–6 with the sentences A–F.

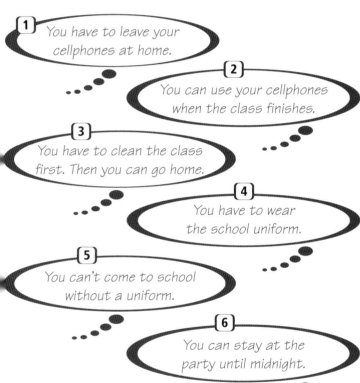

1 You have to leave your cellphones at home.

2 You can use your cellphones when the class finishes.

3 You have to clean the class first. Then you can go home.

4 You have to wear the school uniform.

5 You can't come to school without a uniform.

6 You can stay at the party until midnight.

A She doesn't let us come to class in our own clothes. _5_

B We are allowed to bring cellphones into school. ___

C She makes us clean the class before we leave. ___

D She lets us stay out late. ___

E She makes us wear the school uniform. ___

F We aren't allowed to bring cellphones into school. ___

3 Complete the sentences with the correct form of (*not*) *be allowed to.*

> have   paint   stay up   use   wear

1 I *'m not allowed to stay up* late on weekdays.

2 My parents are very strict. I _____ _____ chat rooms on weekdays.

3 I'm decorating my bedroom. I _____ _____ the walls any color I want.

4 My family loves pets, but we _____ _____ pets in our apartment building.

5 My dad isn't very strict with my brother. He _____ _____ earrings and have tattoos.

4 Fill in the blanks with the correct form of *let* or *make* in the affirmative or negative

1 I have to clean my room.
   My mom _*makes*_ me clean my room.

2 I don't have a safe place to keep my new bike.
   My neighbor _____ me use his garage.

3 I can stay out late on the weekend.
   My dad _____ me stay out late on the weekend.

4 I have to babysit my little brother.
   My parents _____ me babysit my little brother.

Finished?
Page 109, Puzzle 7B

Over to you!

5 Make sentences. Use the following ideas or write your own.

choose your bedtime
wear a fashion (tattoo, hairstyle, jewelry)
have parties at home
help in the house
use chat rooms on the internet

Student A: My parents let me choose my bedtime.
Student B: Really? My parents make me go to bed before 11 p.m.
Student A: I'm not allowed to have a tattoo.
Student B: My parents let me have tattoos.

Living English

Style Wars

Do you want to know how to express yourself and keep your parents happy? Sandy and Cindy have all the answers.

1 I'm a Goth, but I can't dress like a Goth for school, because we aren't allowed to wear makeup to school! It's so unfair! The school lets us wear our own clothes. I can wear black clothes, but it looks stupid without the makeup. *Liam*

2 When I go to a party, my mom makes me wear a dumb dress. She says that "girls should look like girls," but I want to wear my combat pants. My friends' parents let them wear pants to parties, so why can't I? *Mel*

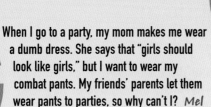

3 I got a piercing in my eyebrow a month ago. My parents were really angry. I don't wear the piercing to school. We aren't allowed to wear jewelry there. But my parents don't let me wear it outside school, either! *Josh*

4 My sister and I are identical twins and our mom makes us dress in EXACTLY the same clothes! We always tell her, "We're individuals," but she doesn't listen. What can we do? We don't have our own money, and my mom doesn't let us go shopping alone. Help!!! *Shona and Sara*

A Ask your parents if you can wear it when you go out. If they don't agree, you'll have to wait until you are older. And next time ask your parents' permission!

B You should explain to your mom that you look the same, but that you have different personalities. Why don't you ask your mom if you can buy just one different outfit? She can give you a budget and you both have to spend the same amount of money.

C You need to express yourself through your clothes, but you can do this outside school. Do you really want to look the same every day? Why don't you wear brighter colors to school? On the weekend you can wear your black clothes and makeup.

D Tell your mom that it's embarrassing to wear different clothes from your friends. Explain that girls can look like girls when they wear pants! Maybe you can wear a T-shirt in a cute color, like pink?

Reading

Before you read

1 Look at the photos and the title. What are the people talking about?

1 problems with relationships
2 problems with school work
3 problems with clothes

While you read

2 Read the text. Match the problems with the advice.

1 _C_   2 ___   3 ___   4 ___

After you read

3 Read the text again. Circle T (True) or F (False).

1 Liam's school lets students wear make-up to school. T / (F)

2 His school makes students wear a uniform. T / F

3 Mel's mom doesn't let her wear pants to parties. T / F

4 Josh is allowed to wear his piercing to school. T / F

5 He isn't allowed to wear his piercing outside school. T / F

6 Shona and Sara's mom doesn't make them wear the same clothes. T / F

Writing

1 Look at the Writing skills box.

2 Write the headings in the correct place.

1 Rules about clothes
2 Rules about behavior
3 General rules

SCHOOL RULES

I go to Greenvale High School. These are our school rules.

A _General rules_

- We aren't allowed to take radios, MP3 players, or cameras to school.
- They make us put our coats in the lockers.
- They let us come into classes when we're late, but they make us sign a "late" book.

B _____

- They make us wear a school uniform.
- We aren't allowed to wear makeup.
- They let us wear small earrings, but we aren't allowed to wear piercings.

C _____

- We aren't allowed to shout.
- We aren't allowed to cheat on tests.
- We aren't allowed to bully other students.

3 Fill in the chart with the information from the text.

	not allowed	let	make
General rules	Carry radios, …		Use lockers
Rules about clothes		Wear small earrings	
Rules about behavior			

4 Now invent some rules you'd like to have at your school. Think of two rules for each section and make notes.

5 Write about your own school rules in exercise 4. Use the text and your notes to help you.

Speaking

1 Listen and read.

2 Look at the Pronunciation box. Listen to the examples.

Pronunciation

Intonation in question tags

If you aren't sure about the answer, your voice goes up (↗) in the tag.

Ecuadorians speak Spanish, don't they?

Listen again and repeat.

3 Match the sentences with the tags.

Sentences

1 Your classmates are from different countries,
2 Your friend has a Saturday job,
3 Your bike is blue,
4 There are three bedrooms in your house,

Tag

A doesn't he?
B aren't there?
C aren't they?
D isn't it?

Listen and check. Then listen and repeat.

4 Listen to the dialogs in exercise 1 again and write an arrow (↗) above each tag. Then practice the dialog with your partner.

5 Change the words in blue. Write a new dialog. Now practice the dialog in class.

Review 7

Vocabulary
Travel essentials

1 Write the object you need next to the problem.

> driver's license   flip-flops   insect spray
> phrase book   scarf   sunblock   vaccination
> wind jacket

1 My brother wants to drive. _driver's license_

2 There's going to be a storm tonight.

   _____

3 I'm traveling to Japan and I can't speak Japanese.

   _____

4 There are big mosquitoes in the jungle.

   _____

5 There is yellow fever in that country.

   _____

6 My neck is cold. _____

7 The sun is really hot today. I don't want to get burned. _____

8 My shoes are too hot for this weather.

   _____

Rules

2 Unscramble the words below.

1 yeob userl _obey rules_

2 cerptes _____

3 akbre lersu _____

4 tirtcs _____

5 eb belsernipos _____

6 yuglibln _____

Grammar
Question tags

1 Write the question tag.

1 They speak English in the Bahamas, _don't they_?

2 Tapas is the national dish of Spain, _____?

3 You don't eat meat, _____?

4 Your brother doesn't drive, _____?

5 I'm a good soccer player, _____?

6 She isn't from Vietnam, _____?

make / let / be allowed

2 Rewrite the sentences about a school and its rules. Use _make_, _let_, or _be allowed_.

1 Students have to get up very early.

   (make) _They make students get up early_ .

2 Students can't write in books.

   (not be allowed) _____

   _____ .

3 Students can use all the school facilities.

   (let) _____

   _____ .

4 Students chat with friends or listen to music in the evening.

   (be allowed) _____

   _____ .

5 Students can't choose their subjects.

   (not let) _____

   _____ .

6 Students have to study a lot for tests.

   (make) _____

   _____ .

Study skills

Recording vocabulary

When you make notes for new vocabulary, organize your vocabulary notebook by topics.

Family relationships: _mother, father_, etc.

Verb expressions: _fall in love with, break up_, etc.

1 **Start a new page in your notebook for unit 7. Record five new words.**

Write or draw the meaning of each word. Write an example if necessary.

sociable = likes meeting new people

Use opposites if possible:

shy ≠ sociable

Use your personal dictionary in class and at home.

Life in the future

Grammar: *will / won't*; first conditional
Vocabulary: stages of life; the environment

Introducing the topic

Vocabulary

1 Match the pictures with the verbs and phrases below.

- [3] apply (for a job / to a university)
- [ ] buy a house
- [ ] get married
- [ ] graduate
- [ ] have children
- [ ] open a business
- [ ] retire

🎧 Now listen and repeat.

Recycling

2 Think of five places where people work. Compare your list with the class.

bank, hospital, restaurant, _____,

_____, _____, _____,

_____.

Exploring the topic

Reading

1 Read what the young people say about their futures. Check (✓) the topics they talk about.

- ✓ education
- ☐ family
- ☐ sports
- ☐ homes
- ☐ money
- ☐ tourism

2 🎧 Read and listen to the text. Write the names of the people.

1 ___Stefan___ thinks lots of people will go on vacation in his country.

2 _____ will travel for work.

3 _____ plans to get a university degree in her own country.

4 _____ will have a family after she starts her career.

5 _____ doesn't think she'll stay in New York.

6 _____ will work with tourists.

Ten years from now ...

After I finish high school in two years, I'll probably study medicine at a good university. Maybe I'll apply to some universities in the U.S. or the U.K. I'll probably become a surgeon. I'm sure I'll get married and have a family too. But first I want to have a good career as a doctor.
Magdalena, São Paulo, Brazil

I think a good education will be more important in the future. I'll definitely want to go to a good university, and I'll probably study law. I don't think I'll study in another country. I think it's important to support education in your own country.
Yasmin, Mumbai, India

My favorite sport is baseball. It's a truly international sport. I'm a good player, and I think I'll join a professional team here in Japan. Then I'll travel all over the world with the team. I'll probably retire when I'm thirty, and then I'll become a coach or a manager.
Yoshi, Tokyo, Japan

I think a lot more people will visit our country in the next ten years. I'll definitely get a certificate in English. Then I'll probably get a job in a hotel or become a tour guide. Or maybe I'll open my own business.
Stefan, Sofia, Bulgaria

I'll probably become an interior designer. I'll study at a good school in New York City, and then I'll apply for a job at a big design company. I probably won't stay in New York after I graduate.
Candice, Michigan, U.S.A.

Grammar

will / won't

Making predictions about the future

1 Look at the chart.

Affirmative	Negative
I'll **probably / definitely study** English.	I **probably / definitely won't stay** in New York.

Take note!

I think and *I don't think* always take an affirmative verb.

I think **I'll study** in the U.S.

I don't think **I'll study** in the U.S.

2 Put the words in the correct order.

1 live / will / probably / I / Mexico City / in

   I will probably live in Mexico City .

2 a famous singer / thinks / he / become / will / he

   _____ .

3 definitely / to several universities / I / apply / will

   _____ .

4 be / they / won't / late / probably

   _____ .

5 think / I / go / I / don't / will / to the concert

   _____ .

3 Look at the pictures, then complete the sentences. Use *will* or *won't* and the verbs in parentheses.

1 He definitely *won't get* the job. (get)

2 I don't think Sofia _____
   to the dance. (come)

3 I'm sure he _____
   before he's eighteen. (graduate)

4 They probably _____
   the train. (catch)

5 She thinks her parents _____
   a new house this year. (buy)

6 They probably _____
   more children. (have)

Finished?
Page 109, Puzzle 8A

Over to you!

4

What will your life be like in five years? Write four sentences about your future with *I think*, *I don't think*, *probably* and *definitely*. Tell the class.

I think I'll go to a university.
I'll probably study history.

Building the topic

Vocabulary

1 Match the pictures with the words below.

1	alternative energy	☐	extinct
☐	garbage	☐	population
☐	global warming	☐	fossil fuel
☐	pollution	☐	recycle

🎧 **Now listen and repeat.**

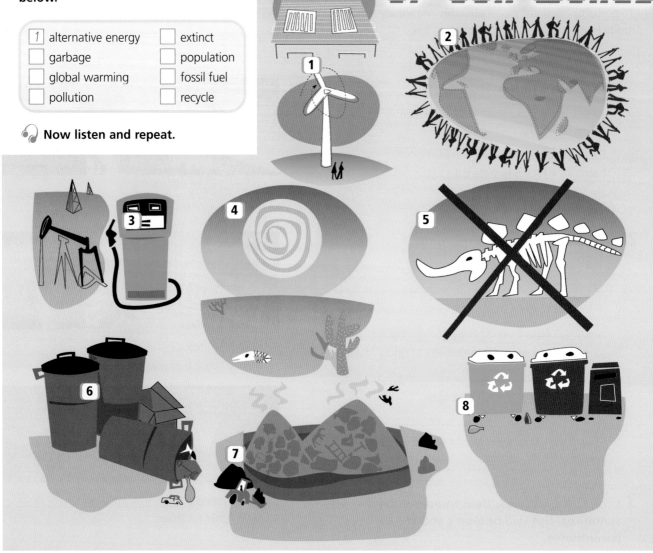

THE FUTURE OF OUR WORLD

2 Read the statements. Match the problems (in red) with the solutions (in green).

Problems

1 "If we throw away all our garbage, we'll create a lot of pollution." _E_
2 "If the population gets bigger, there won't be enough food for everyone." ___
3 "If global warming continues, the oceans will rise and some areas will be under water." ___
4 "If we continue to use fossil fuels, we won't have any fuel in 40 years." ___
5 "If we cut down the trees in the rainforests, a lot of plants and animals will become extinct." ___

Solutions

A "If we develop alternative energy, we won't need fossil fuel."
B "If we grow plants that survive well in hot, dry countries, we'll have enough food."
C "If we stop cutting down trees, a lot of plants and animals will survive."
D "If we save energy, global warming will slow down."
E "If we recycle our paper, plastic and glass, we'll create less pollution."

🎧 **Listen and check.**

Grammar

First conditional

Talking about possible situations and their results

1 Look at the chart.

if clause (simple present)	result clause (*will* / *won't*)
Affirmative	
If we **throw away** all our household waste,	we**'ll create** a lot of pollution.
Negative	
If we **grow** plants that do well in hot, dry countries,	we **won't run** out of food.

2 Find the extra *will* in each sentence and cross it out.

1 If the temperature ~~will~~ becomes warmer, food will be harder to grow.

2 If I will see him, I will tell him your news.

3 If drivers will go too fast, they will get a ticket.

4 If we will drive electric cars, the air will be cleaner.

3 Look at the pictures. Fill in the blanks with the correct form of the verbs in parentheses.

1 If she _falls_ (fall) asleep, she _'ll have_ (have) an accident.

2 If he _____ (practice) more, he _____ _____ (play) for the team.

3 If she _____ (drive) faster, she _____ _____ (not lose) the race.

4 If they _____ (clean up) the river, it _____ (not be) polluted.

5 If they _____ (put out) the fire, it _____ (not destroy) the forest.

6 If you _____ (run), you _____ _____ (catch) the bus.

Finished?
Page 109, Puzzle 8B

Over to you!

4 Say the beginning of a conditional sentence. Can another student complete your sentence? Use the verbs below.

> go shopping   go on vacation
> go out tonight   play video games

Student A: If it rains …
Student B: we'll play video games.

Living English

Futurology

1 Futurologists are professionals who predict the future. Here are some interesting ideas that they have.

1 Will we ever fly on airplanes without pilots?
Air traffic controllers say that it will
5 never happen. If there is an emergency, someone will have to take control of the plane. That will be impossible if there isn't a pilot on it.
10 Some experts think that computers will send information from the plane to air traffic controllers. But if there isn't a pilot, air traffic controllers say that they won't
15 have time to make decisions.

2 Will we have computers in our bodies?
Some people already have small computer chips in
20 their bodies. They save people's lives. For example, they can keep the heart beating. If we have computers in our brains,
25 we'll be more intelligent and we'll have information from all around the world with us all the time.

3 Will books disappear completely?
30 Some experts say "yes" and some say "no". Some of them think that we won't have paper books in the future. If you want to read a book, you'll just download it onto your portable
35 reader. Some portable readers will be waterproof so you can read in the bath! Some people think reading will lose its magic. They love the look, feel and smell of real books, and they
40 also like making notes on the pages!"

Reading 🎧

Before you read

1 Match the pictures with the questions in the text.

1 _C_   2 ___   3 ___

While you read

2 Look at the Reading skills box.

Reading skills

Subject reference

Very often a text will use a noun first, then use *it* or *they* to refer to the noun after that.

John and Tim play <u>tennis</u>. **It** is their favorite sport.
"It" in the second sentence refers to tennis, not to John or Tim.

Read the text and find these pronouns in the text. What do they refer to? Circle a or b.

1 they (line 2):   a ideas   (b) futurologists
2 it (line 9):   a the plane b the air traffic controllers
3 they (line 14): a pilots   b air traffic controllers
4 They (line 20): a computer chips b people
5 it (line 34):   a a book   b a portable reader
6 They (line 38): a people   b portable readers

After you read

3 Read the article again. Fill in the blanks with the words below.

air traffic controllers   chips   download   intelligent
pilot   waterproof

1 If there is an emergency on a plane, you'll always need a _____pilot_____.
2 People say that computers in our brains will make us more _____.
3 If you use a portable reader, you'll _____ books from a computer.
4 The _____ will receive information from the computer about the plane.
5 There are computer _____ in some people's bodies to keep them alive.
6 It won't be a problem if your portable reader gets wet. It will be _____ .

Listening

1 Listen once. What subject are they discussing?

1 Kathy's new job
2 Kathy's future
3 Kathy's new friend

What are two possibilities that Kathy mentions?

2 Listen to the conversation again. Match the beginnings and endings of the sentences.

1 If Kathy does well in college, _D_
2 If Kathy gets a journalism degree, ___
3 If she gets a degree in teaching, ___
4 If she finds a job in New York, ___
5 If she likes her job, ___

A she'll work in a high school.
B she won't go back to live in Boston.
C she'll get a job on a magazine or newsaper.
D she'll have a good job in 10 years.
E she'll stay there.

Writing

1 Read this student's essay about the future. Does she know what she will do?

MY FUTURE
I'm fifteen years old. I'm not really sure what my future will be like. I think I'll apply to schools in the U.S. or in Europe. I'll probably study computer science or history. If I study computer science, I'll probably get a good job.

After I finish my education, I'll definitely come back to my hometown, Managua. I think I'll get married in my twenties. If I get married, I'm sure I'll have kids. I don't think I'll be rich, but I'll probably have a comfortable life.

Andrea L.

2 Fill in the chart with information about Andrea.

Education and work	apply to schools in U.S. / Europe
Personal	

3 Now make notes about what your future will be like.

4 Write an essay about your future. Use the text and your notes to help you.

Review 8

Vocabulary

Stages of life

1 Match the statements 1–7 with the expressions A–G.

1 "I'll probably have three: two girls and a boy." _E_

2 "I'm looking for one in the country, with lots of bedrooms and a big yard." ___

3 "I'll spend my time reading and traveling." ___

4 "I'm so excited about getting my degree!" ___

5 "I want to have my own restaurant." ___

6 "I sent the forms to six different places, but I haven't heard anything yet." ___

7 "We've planned a big wedding." ___

A apply (for a job / to a university)
B buy a house
C get married
D graduate
E have children
F open a business
G retire

The environment

2 Fill in the blanks in these words with vowels.

1 r _e_ cycl _e_   6 _lt _ rn _ t _ v _
2 f_ss_l f__l   _n _ rgy
3 p_p_l_t__n   7 g_rb_g_
4 gl_b_l w_rm_ng   8 p_ll_t__n
5 _xt_nct

Grammar

will / won't

1 Write sentences about these people's future.

1 Pedro / definitely / go / to college
   Pedro will definitely go to college .

2 Juanita / probably / not go / to the U.S.
   _____ .

3 Sandra / probably / become / a doctor
   _____ .

4 Nico / definitely / not play / professional soccer
   _____ .

5 Teresa / definitely / try / to help poor people
   _____ .

First conditional

2 Fill in the blanks. Use the the correct form of the words below.

> create   drive   make   think   use

1 If we recycle glass and metal, _we'll create_ less waste.

2 If we _____ water carefully, we'll have enough for everyone.

3 If we plant more trees, we _____ the air cleaner.

4 If we _____ our cars only for important journeys, we'll save fuel.

5 If we _____ more about the environment, we'll make the world a better place.

Reading

1 Read the text and circle T (True) or F (False).

YOUNG PEOPLE'S VIEW OF THE FUTURE OF TECHNOLOGY

In a recent survey, young people in the U.S. were asked about the future of technology. Here are the results of the survey.

Thirty-three percent of U.S. teenagers believe that gasoline cars will disappear by the year 2015. Twenty-six percent think there won't be any CDs in the next ten years, and twenty-two percent don't think desktop computers will be around for long. Most young people in the survey think there will be technology to solve the world's problems. They think world hunger, disease, and pollution will become things of the past.

However, these young people say they won't study science and technology, and they don't think they'll play a part in solving the world's problems.

1 Thirty-three per cent of U.S. teenagers think we won't have gasoline cars by 2015. T / F

2 The young people think we'll have CDs in 2016. T / F

3 They think there won't be any problems like hunger, disease and pollution. T / F

4 The young people all want to study science and technology at college. T / F

5 The young people will help find solutions to world problems. T / F

9 A star is made

Grammar: passive (simple present); passive (simple past)
Vocabulary: TV shows; growing up

ntroducing the topic

Vocabulary

1 Match the pictures with the words below.

5 audience	audition	contestant
host	judges	prize
recording contract		TV viewer

🎧 Now listen and repeat.

Recycling

2 Make a list of jobs that famous people do.

actor, _____, _____,

_____, _____, _____

Exploring the topic

How to become an American Idol

American Idol is a show where talent is recognized and music careers are made. The big prize is a recording contract and instant fame. Here's what you do to become an American Idol.

First of all, auditions are organized around the United States. Thousands of hopeful young people sing in front of the judges. After several days, two hundred singers are selected to go on to the next stage of the contest.

Finally, twenty-four contestants are chosen. Twelve men and twelve women are taken to Hollywood. This is when things start to get serious. For three weeks, each singer has to perform for about a minute. They're watched by the same three judges, and by millions of TV viewers. The best singers aren't chosen by the judges. The TV viewers vote for the contestant they like best. The two singers with the lowest number of votes sing one last time, and then they're sent home.

When there are only twelve contestants, they're given the chance to work with famous musicians and songwriters. They're also given new hairstyles, makeup, and clothes.

The voting continues until there are only two contestants in the competition. Now it's time for the final. The final isn't held in the TV studio, it's held in a big theater with a very large audience. The votes are counted, and the new American Idol is announced. After that, a tour is organized for the top ten contestants, and they visit cities all over the U.S.

Reading

1 Have you ever heard of *American Idol*? Do you have similar shows in your country?

2 🎧 Read and listen to the article. How many contestants go to Hollywood? How many are in the final show?

3 Circle T (True) or F (False).

1 After the auditions, there are two hundred contestants. T / F

2 The judges choose the best singers. T / F

3 The contestants get to work with famous singers. T / F

4 In the last program, there are only two contestants. T / F

5 Twenty contestants go on tour after the show finishes. T / F

Grammar

Passive (simple present)

Talking about processes

1 Look at the chart.

Passive (simple present)
be + past participle
One contestant **is sent** home.
Auditions **are organized**.
The singers **aren't chosen** by the judges.
The finale **isn't held** in a TV studio.

2 Fill in the blanks with the correct form of *be*, affirmative.

1 Great musicians __are__ often discovered in small music clubs.

2 The film _____ shown three times a day in this movie theater.

3 Photographers take many photos for a news story. The photos _____ printed in newspapers.

4 This TV show _____ shown live.

5 This prize _____ given once a year to the best dancer in the school.

6 Many old songs _____ recorded by new singers.

3 Complete the passive sentences about a fashion show. Use the verbs in parentheses.

1 A venue for the show ____is chosen____. (choose)

2 The clothes _____. (make)

3 Models _____ for the show. (hire)

4 The invitations _____. (print)

5 Music _____ for the show. (select)

6 At the end of the show, the designer _____. (introduce)

Take note!

In many passive sentences, we don't know who does the action. To say who does the action, we add *by* + the agent.

The singers are coached.

The singers are coached **by famous musicians**.

4 Write sentences in the passive to describe how CDs are made.

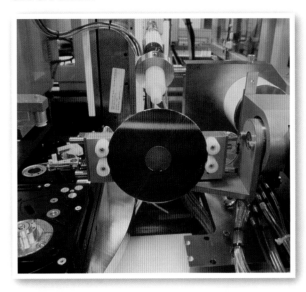

1 new songs / write / by the musicians

  New songs are written by the musicians.

2 the best songs / choose / by the group

  _____.

3 a lot of songs / record / in the studio

  _____.

4 the recording / approve / by the producers

  _____.

5 thousands of CDs / produce / in the factory

  _____.

6 the CDs / sell / in the music stores

  _____.

Finished?
Page 109, Puzzle 9A

Over to you!

5 Write three false sentences about your school. Use the ideas below. Ask the class to correct the sentences.

tests / write
new teachers / hire
classrooms / clean
soccer team / train
English / teach
homework / do

Student A: The tests are written by the students.
Student B: No. The tests are written by the teachers.

9 A star is made

Building the topic

Carlos Acosta
Accidental Ballet Star

Carlos Acosta was born in 1973 in Havana, Cuba. He was from a poor family. His father was a truck driver, and there were eleven children in the family. Carlos was a difficult child and he got into a lot of trouble. Carlos was sent to a very strict school by his father. It was a ballet school. He was nine years old.

At first, Carlos hated the school. He was bullied by the other kids. He wanted to be a professional soccer player. He skipped classes to play soccer, and he was expelled from the school twice. His father spoke to the director of the school, and the school took Carlos back. When he was 13, he saw the National Ballet of Cuba. After that, he started to work hard and his dancing improved a lot. At the age of sixteen, he won an award for the best boy ballet dancer in the world.

He joined the English National Ballet when he was eighteen, and then he started dancing for the National Ballet of Cuba. Other young dancers from Cuba were inspired by his life story. Carlos became a national hero. People now think Carlos Acosta is one of the greatest dancers in the world.

Vocabulary

1 **Read the text. Then fill in the blanks with the words below.**

> got into trouble   improved   skipped (classes)
> was bullied   was expelled   were inspired

1 People were angry with him because he did something bad.
   He _got into trouble_ .

2 He had to leave school because he did something bad.
   He _____ .

3 He became better at dancing.
   His dancing _____ .

4 He was an example to young Cuban dancers.
   They _____ by him.

5 He stayed away from school without permission.
   He _____ classes.

6 Other children hurt him.
   He _____ .

🎧 **Now listen and repeat.**

2 🎧 **Read and listen to the text. Answer the questions.**

1 Where was Carlos born? ___Cuba___

2 What year was Carlos born? _____

3 How many brothers and sisters did he have?
   _____

4 Did he choose to go to ballet school? _____

5 What prize did he get when he was sixteen?
   _____

6 What did he do when he was eighteen?
   _____

Grammar

Passive (simple past)

Talking about events in the past

1 Look at the chart.

Passive (simple past)
was / were + past participle
He **was sent** to ballet school.
He **wasn't bullied** by the other kids.
Other young dancers **were inspired** by his story.

2 Circle *was* or *were*.

1 Andy (was) / were invited to play on a professional basketball team.

2 Tim and Frank was / were expelled from school.

3 Tamsin was / were chosen to sing at the school concert.

4 My parents was / were asked to a party.

5 I was / were helped with my homework.

3 Complete the sentences. Use the passive form in the past and the verbs in parentheses.

1 Our car _____ *was stolen* _____ yesterday. Now we have to take the bus! (steal)

2 Cordelia _____ the prize for Best Young Artist of the Year. (give)

3 I auditioned for the play, and I _____ for the part I wanted. (not choose)

4 Malcolm got good grades on his test. He _____ _____ at medical college. (accept)

5 Amit and Dahlia _____ on the radio. (interview)

6 Kelly cheated on a test. She _____ from her school. (expel)

4 Look at the picture. Write sentences in the simple past passive.

1 the window / break / by the thieves
   The window was broken by the thieves .

2 the painting / steal
   _____ .

3 they / film / by security cameras
   _____ .

4 they / see / by the cleaner
   _____ .

5 the thieves / arrest / by the police
   _____ .

6 the painting / return / to the museum
   _____ .

Finished?
Page 109, Puzzle 9B

Over to you!

5 Write five passive statements for a True or False quiz. Use the verbs below. Test your classmates.

> break (a record)   score   sing   win   write

Student A: The song *One* was sung by Mary J. Blige.
Student B: False.
Student A: No, it's true. The 2006 World Cup was won by ...

Living English

Manufactured Pop

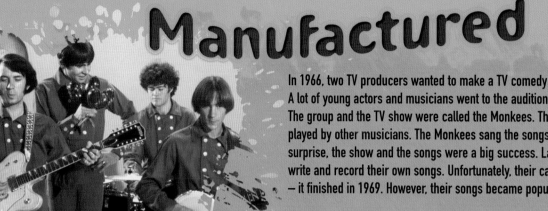

In 1966, two TV producers wanted to make a TV comedy show about a pop group. A lot of young actors and musicians went to the auditions, and four were hired. The group and the TV show were called the Monkees. The songs were written and played by other musicians. The Monkees sang the songs on the show. To everyone's surprise, the show and the songs were a big success. Later on, the group began to write and record their own songs. Unfortunately, their career as a group was short — it finished in 1969. However, their songs became popular again in the 1980s.

In 1994, five young women answered an advertisement in a newspaper in England for a girl band. They became the Spice Girls. But they soon argued with their manager. He wanted them all to look the same, but the Spice Girls wanted to look different. They found another manager. He let them create their own look and sound. They became a huge success around the world. Their career was also short, but they're still remembered. One of the Spice Girls, Victoria, married the soccer player David Beckham!

In the past, most bands started their music careers as a group of friends. They started playing in small clubs, and after a lot of hard work, they became famous. However, some groups didn't do this. They were "manufactured" by the pop industry. Here are two examples:

Reading 🎧

Before you read

1 **Look at the title and the photos. What do you think the article is about?**

1 making music CDs
2 making a pop group

While you read

2 **Read the article once. Write the names of the groups. Then find the number of people in each group, and the year when it started.**

1 name: _____

number: _____

year: _____

2 name: _____

number: _____

year: _____

After you read

3 **Read the article again. Write the names of the groups next to the statements.**

1 They didn't play their own instruments at first.
   The Monkees

2 They didn't like their first manager.
   _____

3 They didn't want to look the same.
   _____

4 Their group was hired for a TV show.
   _____

5 They answered an advertisement in a newspaper.
   _____

6 People listened to their music in the 1980s.
   _____

Listening 🎧

1 Listen to the conversation once. Who are they talking about? What is he going to do?

2 Listen to the conversation again. Circle T (True) or F (False).

1 Adam has just had an accident. T / (F)

2 Adam is going to take part in a reality show. T / F

3 The idea of the show is to make people believe something that is untrue. T / F

4 If people believe you, you become a pop singer. T / F

5 Adam is going to pretend to be a dancer. T / F

6 Adam knows the exact date of the show. T / F

Writing

1 Read the description about choosing a cheerleading squad. How many steps are there?

CHOOSING CHEERLEADERS
by Neela

Here's how cheerleaders are chosen at our school.

● _____, applications are sent in. Photos of the girls and boys are attached to the applications.

● _Then_ the applicants are interviewed by two teachers and two cheerleaders.

● _____, auditions are held. Applicants are judged on their skills, appearance and personality.

● _____, we make our decisions. A vote is taken.

● _____, the new squad is announced. Practices begin.

2 Look at the Writing skills box.

Writing skills

First, then, next, after that, finally

We use *first, next, after that, then,* and *finally* to sequence events.

First, the competitors went to the audition. **Then** the competitors sang in front of the judges. **Next,** TV viewers voted for the best song. **After that,** the host gave the prize to the winner. **Finally,** the winner recorded a song.

3 Read Neela's description again. Fill in the blanks with these sequencing words.

Next   First   Finally   Then   After that

4 Fill in the chart with the missing steps from Neela's description.

Cheerleading squad	School play
● *take applications*	● Students and teachers choose play
● *interview applicants*	● hold auditions
●	● make costumes
●	● hold rehearsals
●	● perform the play

5 Look at the steps for putting on a school play.

6 Write a description about putting on a school play. Use sequencing words and the chart to help you.

Review 9

Vocabulary

TV shows

1 Find eight words about TV talent shows.

Growing up

2 Fill in the blanks with the words below.

> was bullied   was expelled   got into trouble
> improved   were inspired   skipped

1 Many young people _____ were inspired _____ to play golf by Tiger Woods.

2 John's singing was terrible, but now he has lessons and he's _____ a lot.

3 The students _____ science class.

4 Vera is unhappy. She _____ by some older kids at school today.

5 Martina was very rude and _____. She had to stay late at school.

6 David _____ from school because he stole some money.

Grammar

Passive (simple present)

1 Write the sentences in the present simple passive.

1 The school magazine _____ is written _____ by students. (write)

2 Prizes _____ every year. (not award)

3 New players _____ by coaches. (choose)

4 The best projects _____ by the teachers. (display)

5 His stories _____ by a lot of people. (not read)

Passive (simple past)

2 Complete the story. Use the verbs in parentheses in the past simple passive.

> One day, Danny and Susan (1) _____ were called _____ (call) to their boss's office. They (2) _____ _____ (tell) to drive to an office on the other side of town. They (3) _____ (not tell) why they had to go there. When they got to the office, they waited in a small room for an hour. Then Danny (4) _____ (take) to a conference room by an assistant. When the door opened, Danny heard people shouting "Happy birthday!" and he (5) _____ (give) a present. His boss, Susan, and his co-workers were all there. Cake and ice cream (6) _____ (serve) and everyone had a great time.

10 Relationships

Grammar: verbs + prepositions; infinitive or *-ing*
Vocabulary: relationships; plans and opinions

Introducing the topic

Vocabulary

1 Match the pictures with the words below.

- [4] make up with
- [ ] get divorced from
- [ ] have an argument with
- [ ] break up with
- [ ] fall in love with
- [ ] get married to

🎧 Now listen and repeat.

Recycling

2 Match the verbs with the speech bubbles.

1 introduce _c_
2 meet ___
3 get to know ___
4 keep in touch ___
5 invite on a date ___

a Tell me all about yourself.

b Will you go out with me this weekend?

c Fred, meet my friend Emma.

d Hi! How are you?

e Will you call me soon? I want to hear your news.

Exploring the topic

TV SOAPS

This is what happened in last week's soaps.

BIG VIEW MOUNTAIN

A lot of people were talking about Pete and Tanisha at the end of the last episode. They were seen shopping together on Fifth Avenue – in a jewelry store! Will he ask her to get married to him? People were talking about Pete's sister Marnie too. Somebody saw her with the new boy from school. She really likes him. He's going to meet her family. But what will her father think of him?

LIFE NYC

In last week's episode, Tom had an argument with Katie. They can't decide which college to go to. Will Katie break up with Tom and go to California to study, or will Tom make up with her? And what about Clarissa? Her parents, Joe and Imelda, had another big argument last week. Will Imelda get divorced from Joe? Who will Clarissa live with?

EVERGREEN PLACE

A year ago, Tina got married to Zeke. In last week's episode, Tina introduced her new friend Maria to Zeke. Big mistake! Maria falls in love with every boy she meets. Will Maria try to steal Zeke from Tina?

Reading

1 Read the text. Answer the questions.

1 Who is Tom's girlfriend? _Katie_____

2 Who are Clarissa's mother and father?
_____

3 Who is Tanisha's boyfriend? _____

4 Who is Marnie? _____

5 Who is Zeke's wife? _____

6 Who is Maria? _____

2 🎧 Read and listen to the text. Write the names of the shows next to the statements.

1 There will probably be a wedding soon.
_Big View Mountain_____

2 Two people had an argument about college.
_____

5 A woman thinks that her friend might steal her husband. _____

4 Someone has a new boyfriend.
_____

3 A girl is worried about where she's going to live.
_____

Grammar

Verbs + prepositions
Talking about relationships

1 Look at the chart.

Affirmative and negative			
Tina	**got married**	**to**	her boyfriend.
Tom	didn't **make up**	**with**	Katie.

2 Circle the correct preposition.

1 Do you think Jason is going to make up about / **(with)** Kelly?
2 Cameron got divorced with / from Casie.
3 James fell in love with / about Mei at a party.
4 Mark had an argument of / with his girlfriend.
5 Jessica broke up from / with Keeler.

3 Look at the pictures from a soap opera below. Write sentences in the simple past. Use the correct prepositions.

1 Heidi / fall in love / Peter
  Heidi fell in love with Peter .

2 Heidi / break up / Eric
  _____ .

3 Heidi / get married / Peter
  _____ .

4 Heidi / have an argument / Peter
  _____ .

5 Heidi / get divorced / Peter
  _____ .

6 Heidi / make up / Eric
  _____ .

4 Look at the chart.

Questions
Who will Clarrisa live **with**?
Who will Tanisha get married **to**?

5 Put the words in order to make questions.

1 talk / he / who / did / to
  Who did he talk to ?

2 have an argument with / Maria / did / who
  _____ ?

3 what / talk / did / you / about
  _____ ?

4 complain / Dana / who / did / about
  _____ ?

5 he / go out / did / who / with
  _____ ?

Finished?
Page 111, Puzzle 10A

Over to you!

6 Invent a story in class. Take turns to add new sentences. Use the verbs from page 81.

Student A: Manuela and Juan fell in love …
Student B: They got married in Paris …

Building the topic

ARE YOU A PARENT'S DREAM OR A PARENT'S NIGHTMARE? DO THE QUIZ TO FIND OUT.

Dilemma 1

You've arranged to go to a party with a boy that your parents don't like. They can't stand seeing you with this boy, but you really like him. What do you do?

a I don't go to the party because I don't want to fight with my parents.

b I arrange a dinner. That way my parents can get to know him better.

c I go to the party and I don't tell my parents!

Dilemma 2

You've decided to go to a college far away from your home town. You don't mind living on your own, but your family keeps asking you to stay in your home town. What do you do?

a I agree to stay in my home town, but I'm very unhappy.

b I talk to my parents and explain that I really want to be independent.

c I don't tell them my plans. I'm old enough to decide my own future.

Dilemma 3

You're a good student, but you're bored with school. You aren't interested in going to classes. You plan to leave school and work as a builder. Your parents think you should finish high school first. What do you do?

a I finish high school and I promise to work hard.

b I get information about building courses. My parents can then see that I am serious about it.

c I leave school. My parents are too old-fashioned.

Vocabulary

1 Read the quiz and answer the questions.

2 Fill in the blanks with the words below.

> arrange   can't stand   decided   keeps
> mind   interested in   promise

1 I'm not _interested in_ studying math. It's boring.

2 Mom, I will clean my room tonight. I _____ to do it.

3 I _____ listening to rock music. It's too loud.

4 Let's _____ to see a movie next week.

5 I don't _____ cutting the grass.

6 We've _____ to go to Singapore on vacation.

7 My sister always steals my clothes. She _____ wearing them to parties.

🎧 **Now listen and repeat.**

Now count how many a, b or c answers you have.
Mostly a: You're a parent's dream.
Mostly b: Keep trying.
Mostly c: You're a parent's nightmare!

3 🎧 **Read and listen to the quiz. Write the number of the dilemma.**

1 You don't like school and you want to work. ___

2 Your parents don't like your date. ___

3 You want to study in another town. ___

Grammar

Infinitive or -ing

Talking about plans and opinions

1 Look at the chart.

verb + *to* + infinitive	
decide	I **decided to stay** in my home town.
arrange	I've **arranged to go** to a party.
promise	You **promise to work** hard.

2 Fill in the blanks. Use the words in parentheses and the infinitive. Use the simple past.

1 I ___arranged to see___ (arrange / see) my Canadian friend in Toronto last week.

2 My sister _____ (want / go) to a party yesterday, but she was ill.

3 My friend from Italy _____ (promise / come) to my party.

4 Tim _____ (agree / do) the work by next week.

5 My mom_____ (decide / lend) me her a car for the weekend.

3 Look at the chart.

verb + *-ing*	
can't stand	They **can't stand seeing** me with this guy.
keep	My parents **keep asking** me to stay.
mind	I **don't mind living** on my own.
not interested in	I'm **not interested in going** to classes.

4 Fill in the blanks. Use the words in parentheses and the *-ing* form of the verbs below.

1 Do you ___enjoy going___ to the movie theater? (enjoy / go)

2 They _____ their homework. (can't stand / do)

3 I don't _____ during summer vacation. (mind / work)

4 Are you going to _____ English on your vacation? (practice / speak)

5 He's going to travel around the world. He _____ about other cultures. (enjoy / learn)

5 Correct the mistakes.

1 Do you promise finish your homework?
   Do you promise to finish your homework ?

2 I don't mind wash the car.
   _____ ?

3 I can't stand play soccer.
   _____ ?

4 Do you usually want go out with friends on the weekend? _____
   _____ ?

5 I keep lose my keys.
   _____ ?

6 Bianca enjoys meet new people.
   _____ ?

Finished?
Page 111, Puzzle 10B

Over to you!

6 Write sentences. Use these ideas. Compare your sentences in class.

go on vacation
tell the truth
take exams
wait for people
listen to my friend's secrets
argue with my parents
talk about my feelings

Me
_____

I want to talk about my feelings.

I don't mind changing plans.

I enjoy ...

I can't stand ...

Living English

SIGNS OF ATTRACTION

First impressions are an important start to any new relationship, but can you read the signs? Is it just friendship or a real attraction? Here are some tips to help you.

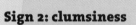

Sign 1: eye contact
You look at each other when you're speaking. This means you feel relaxed and comfortable. It also shows sincerity and trust. Keeping eye contact is a sign of interest. It means you both want to be there, and enjoy each other's company and conversation.

Sign 2: clumsiness
You're clumsy. You drop your keys, fall over things, and spill your drink during a conversation. Why? You're nervous. But don't feel bad. Being clumsy is a good sign. It means you really like the other person.

Sign 3: agreeing

You agree to do things that you don't like to do. For example, you agree to go to a hard rock concert and you can't stand listening to hard rock. Or you say yes to sharing a salad, but you hate vegetables! Great sign! You want to share the other person's world and enjoy the things that they like.

Sign 4: uniqueness
You notice the smallest details about the other person, and you like them. Your date's hairstyle looks great, and his clothes are the best. Maybe they're not fashionable, but they're perfect on him. Even your least favorite color looks fantastic.

Sign 5: brightness
Has someone switched on the lights? The room looks brighter. This happens because when you look at something or someone that causes positive feelings, the pupils in your eyes become bigger and everything looks brighter.

Sign 6: familiarity
You think you've known each other for a long time. You find out that you enjoy doing the same things. You listen to the same music, you're good at the same sports, and you even like eating the same foods. You don't notice other people or things around you.

Reading 🎧

Before you read

1 Do you think you always know when someone is the "right" person for you? Why / Why not?

While you read

2 Read the text. Check (✔) the subjects in the text.
1 physical appearance
2 hobbies
3 music
4 clothes
5 TV
6 school
7 food

After you read

3 Read the article again. Write the name of the signs next to the statements.
1 You have a lot of small accidents. _clumsiness_
2 You have the same interests. _____
3 Everything looks clearer and lighter. _____
4 You look at the other person's eyes a lot. _____
5 You love your date's style. _____
6 You want to do things you don't normally do. _____

Listening 🎧

1 Look at the Listening skills box.

Listening skills

Listening for key words

Key words are usually nouns, verbs, or adjectives. They give you the most important imformation.

2 Listen to the dialogs. Check (✓) the words you hear.

break up with

getting married

getting divorced

fallen in love

make up with

had an argument

3 Check (✓) the correct option.

a   The dialogs are about dating.

b   The dialogs are about friendship.

4 Listen to the three dialogs again. Match the dialogs 1–3 with the descriptions A–C.

Dialog 1 ____

Dialog 2 ____

Dialog 3 ____

A   breaking up

B   getting married

C   falling in love

Speaking 🎧

1 Listen and read.

2 Look at the Pronunciation box. Listen to the examples.

Pronunciation

Responding to news

Our voice goes up (↗) when we respond to good news. It goes down (↘) when we respond to bad news.

That's great!   That's terrible!

Listen again and repeat.

3 Listen to the dialogs. Check (✓) the phrases for good news. Put a cross (✗) next to the phrases for bad news.

1   That's great. ✓   4   That's gross. ____

2   That's horrible. ____   5   That's beautiful. ____

3   That's wonderful. ____

Now listen and repeat.

4 Practice the dialog with a partner.

5 Look at the words in blue. Write a new dialog. Now practice the dialog in class.

Review 10

Vocabulary

Relationships

1 Write the expressions below in the chart.

> break up with   fall in love with
> get divorced from   get married to
> have an argument with   make up with

starting a relationship	ending a relationship
	break up with

Plans and opinions

2 Fill in the blanks with the words below.

> arranged   can't stand   decide   keeps   mind
> interested in   promised

Jack is a bad student. He (1) _can't stand_ doing his homework. He hates it! He (2) _____ skipping class. He does it every day! Jack isn't (3) _____ math and science class. He thinks they're boring. He doesn't (4) _____ sports. They're OK. In fact, Jack really loves baseball and he's (5) _____ to join the school team. He's (6) _____ to speak to the coach tomorrow, and he's (7) _____ to train hard every day.

Grammar

Verbs + prepositions

1 Correct the mistake in the sentences.

1   Mario is always complaining of school homework. _about_

2   Gina is tired about getting up early. _____

3   Jane had an argument on Sam. _____

4   I think Jude will make up on Luisa. _____

5   The teacher is talking of tonight's homework. _____

2 Write the questions for the sentences in exercise 1.

1   _What is Mario always complaining about_ ?

2   _____ ?

3   _____ ?

4   _____ ?

5   _____ ?

Infinitive or -ing

3 Fill in the blanks with the verbs in parentheses.

1   The school principal plans _____ a new gym. (open)

2   Javier has promised _____ the walls. (paint)

4   Four music students are planning _____ a concert. (have)

5   We enjoyed _____ the film. (see)

6   Many students want _____ the school uniform. (change)

Reading

1 Read the text and answer the questions.

> ### Love in cyberspace
>
> Online dating is very popular. It's similar to online shopping, but with online shopping, you get a description, a brand name, and a photo of the product you're interested in. With online dating, there's no brand name, and the description and photo might not be real!
>
> One reader wrote in. "I met the perfect guy online. He was the right age, and he had a great job. He sent me his photo and I thought he was really good-looking. We e-mailed each other for several months. I then suggested a meeting. He didn't want to meet, and I asked him what the problem was. I found out that "he" was a 56-year-old woman. She was writing a book about cyber-romance and she was doing research!"

1   What information do you get with online shopping? _Description, ..._

2   What problems do you get with online dating?

3   Why did the reader want to date the guy she met online?

4   Why didn't the person want to meet the reader?

11 Sports world

Grammar: indefinite pronouns; relative clauses
Vocabulary: sports equipment; sports words

Introducing the topic

1 snorkel
2
3
4
5
6
7
8

Vocabulary

1 Label the pictures with the words below.

> cap   fins   gloves   mask   puck   snorkel
> spikes   stick

🎧 Now listen and repeat.

Recycling

2 Match the sports with the pictures.

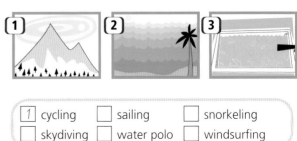

1 2 3

> [1] cycling   ☐ sailing   ☐ snorkeling
> ☐ skydiving   ☐ water polo   ☐ windsurfing

Exploring **the topic**

UNUSUALSPORTS
Your answers to questions about unusual sports.

1 Octopush

It's underwater hockey. I've played this sport in Canada. You push the puck with a stick into the other team's goal. It's not difficult. This is a sport for everyone. You need the right equipment: a snorkel, a mask, gloves, fins, and a cap. You don't need anything else. Is there anywhere you can play this sport in South America? Does anyone know?

2 Bog snorkeling

This sport takes place somewhere in the U.K. People swim in muddy water, wearing a snorkel and fins. Does anyone have any details about this sport? I'd really like to try it.

3 Burling

How about burling? This sport is fun! Two people walk on a log in a river, and they try to push the other person off the log. The first person to fall three times loses the competition. I know you have to wear something on your feet. Does anyone know what that is?

Reply A

Someone in my class does this sport. You wear spikes on your shoes to help you stay on the log. Yes, I agree. It's a great sport.

Reply B

There are clubs and competitions in Brazil, Argentina, Colombia and Venezuela. Has anyone ever played underwater rugby? It's similar.

Reply C

Competitors have to swim 55 meters in the shortest time, and you can only use your fins to swim. Spectators should wear their oldest clothes. Everything ends up dirty!

Reading

1 Read the text. Match the sports 1–3 with the replies A–C.

1 Octopush _B_

2 Bog snorkeling ___

3 Burling ___

2 🎧 Read and listen to the text. Write the sport.

1 You use a puck for this sport. _Octopush_

2 You wear special spikes for this sport. _____

3 You have to score in the other team's goal. _____

4 You wear a mask and a snorkel for this sport. _____

5 This sport is for two people. _____

6 You have to swim very quickly in muddy water. _____

7 This sport is played underwater. _____

8 You fall off a log in this sport. _____

Grammar

Indefinite pronouns

Talking about indefinite people, things, and places

1 Look at the chart.

some – affirmative statements
Someone in my class does this sport.
You have to wear **something** on your feet.
This sport takes place **somewhere** in the U.K.

any – negative and questions
You don't need **anything** else.
Does **anyone** know?
Is there **anywhere** you can play?

every – affirmative statements
This is a sport for **everyone**.
Everything ends up dirty.
There are clubs **everywhere** in the U.S.

Take note!

We use *one* for a person, *thing* for an object, and *where* for a place.

We use singular verbs after all indefinite pronouns.
Everyone **knows** football and basketball.

2 Circle the correct word.

1 There's (someone) / anyone at the door. Who is it?

2 Great. There isn't someone / anyone in the pool.

3 There's anything / something strange in my glass.

4 I've looked for my keys anywhere / everywhere, but I can't find them.

5 I'm bored. I don't have anything / something to do.

6 There's someone / anyone waiting for you.

3 Fill in the blanks with the verb in parentheses in the correct form. Use the affirmative or negative.

1 Let's go to this restaurant. Everywhere else ____is____ (be) crowded.

2 That's strange. There _____ (not be) anyone in class.

3 Someone _____ (want) to speak to you.

4 _____ (be) there anything to eat? I'm hungry.

5 Sara _____ (like) anything in the shop.

6 There _____ (be) something on your T-shirt. Eww. It's a bug!

4 Fill in the blanks with the correct indefinite pronoun.

1 There's ___*something*___ in my shoe.

2 There isn't _____ in this room.

3 _____ is watching TV.

4 _____ is shouting. Who is he?

5 I want to stay at home. I don't want to go _____ .

Finished?
Page 111, Puzzle 11A

Over to you!

5 Think about last weekend. Use the following verbs: *meet, eat, see, visit, listen.* Tell the class. Can the class guess what you did?

Student A: I went somewhere cool last weekend.
Student B: You went to the new dance club.
Student A: Yes!
Student A: I met someone.
Student B: You met a famous person.
Student A: No, I met your sister!

Building the topic

SPORTSTRIVIA

Do you think you know a lot about sports?
Test your knowledge and try our quiz.

TENNIS

Tennis is a sport that is popular all over the world. But did you know that tennis was originally played with the hand, not with a racket? The game was called "jeu de paume" (game of the palm).

1 paddle

1 ___France___ is the country where tennis started.

　a England　(b) France

2 _____ were the people who first played tennis. They played it on indoor courts in the 12th century.

　a monks　b kings

3 _____ was the equipment that people first used to hit the ball.

　a A paddle　b A racket

4 At first, the _____ were about one and a half meters high. Now they're just over one meter high.

　a goal posts　b nets

RUGBY FOOTBALL

The person who started rugby football was sixteen-year-old William Webb Ellis. He played soccer at school, but he didn't like the rules. One day, in 1823, he was playing a game on the school soccer field, when he took the ball with his hands, and ran with it. And rugby was born!

5 _____ was the country where the game started.

　a New Zealand　b England

6 _____ were the places where people started to play rugby.

　a schools　b streets

7 The ball which they used was made from _____.

　a a part of an animal　　b rubber

8 _____ is the person who controls a game of rugby.

　a a referee　　b an umpire

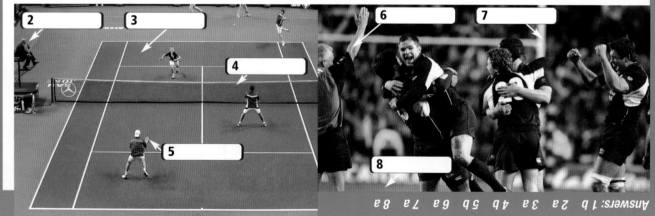

2　3

4

5

6　7

8

Answers: 1 b　2 a　3 a　4 b　5 b　6 a　7 a　8 a

Vocabulary

1 Label the photos with the words below.

> court　field　goal posts　net　paddle
> racket　referee　umpire

🎧 Now listen and repeat.

2 Read the quiz and answer the questions. Then check your answers.

3 🎧 Read and listen to the quiz. Correct the wrong information.

1　Tennis originated in ~~New Zealand~~. *France*

2　<u>English</u> monks first played tennis with their hands.

3　People first played tennis with a <u>racket</u>.

4　William Webb Ellis was the person who invented the game of <u>tennis</u>.

5　Rugby first started in the <u>U.S.</u>

6　An umpire controls the game of <u>rugby</u>.

Grammar
Relative pronouns
Defining people, things, and places

1 Look at the chart.

who
William Webb Ellis was a person. He invented rugby.
William Webb Ellis was **the person who** invented rugby.

which / that
Tennis is a sport. It's popular all over the world.
Tennis is **a sport that** is popular all over the world.
They used the ball. It was made from part of an animal.
The ball which they used was made from part of an animal.

where
France is a country. Tennis originated in France.
France was **the country where** tennis started.

2 Read the definitions. Circle the correct relative pronoun.

1 A court is a place where / who people play ball games like tennis.

2 A referee is the person which / who controls games like soccer and basketball.

3 A field is a place that / where people play baseball and soccer.

4 A net is a thing which / where is in the center of the court.

5 The goal posts are things that / where are part of the goal.

6 The umpire is the person where / who controls games like baseball and tennis.

3 Fill in the blanks with the correct relative pronoun: *who, where,* or *which*.

1 This is the town _____ I live. It's quiet and there are a lot of parks.

2 My house is the one _____ is made of stone and dark wood.

3 The person _____ lives next door is my best friend.

4 This is the café _____ my friends and I meet every evening.

5 That is the bus _____ takes me to school every day.

4 Complete the sentences. Use relative clauses.

1 This is the gym. We play volleyball here.
This is the place _where we play volleyball_ .

2 Tim is the trainer. He makes us train very hard.
Tim is someone _____
_____ .

3 This is the music room. We play instruments here.
This is the place _____
_____ .

4 This is the piano. I play it at school concerts.
This is something _____
_____ .

5 Fred is a young man. He teaches us music.
Fred is someone _____
_____ .

Finished?
Page 111, Puzzle 11B

Over to you!

5 Write a definition. Can the class guess the word?

Student A: It's someone who fixes cars.
Student B: Mechanic.
Student A: Right.
Student A: It's something that cuts food.
Student B: Knife.
Student A: Yes!

Living English

AN OLYMPIC LIFE
Jim Thorpe (1887–1953)

Jim Thorpe was born in Oklahoma in 1887. He was half American, half Native American. His family was poor and life was hard, but Thorpe was very good at sports. From a young age, he played football, baseball, and lacrosse. By the age of 22, he was playing semi-professional baseball and he got some money for this.

Thorpe competed in the 1912 Olympic Games in Sweden when he was 24. He won gold medals and set world records. However, the Olympic games were only for amateurs. Amateurs didn't receive money for their sport. The Olympic committee thought that Thorpe was a professional athlete because he received money when he was 22. Thorpe had to give back his medals.

However, Thorpe soon became a successful athlete. He played for the New York Giants baseball team, and six professional football teams. He earned a lot of money and became very popular. In 1950, he was named "the greatest American football player and greatest male athlete". He retired at the age of 41, but continued to be active, and started to play another sport, basketball.

Outside sports, he found it hard to find work. He had eight children to support, and life was difficult. Although he didn't have much money, he enjoyed life with his wife, Patricia. He died at the age of 66. Thorpe was awarded the title Athlete Of The Century. Thirty years after his death, his gold medals were given back to his family.

Reading 🎧

Before you read

1 Do you like the Olympic Games? What do you know about them?

While you read

2 Read the text. Match the two halves of the sentences.

1 His childhood was hard, but ___

2 He was good at track events, but ___

3 He won Olympic awards, but ___

4 He didn't have any money, but ___

A he was happy.

B he had to return them.

C he showed he had a great talent for sports.

D he could also play football and baseball.

After you read

3 Read the text again and order the events.

a He showed a talent for football and for track and field sports at school. ___

b He retired from sports. ___

c He gave his Olympic medals back. ___

d He was born in Oklahoma in 1887. _1_

e He was named the greatest American football player and athlete. ___

f Jim Thorpe set Olympic records and won gold medals. ___

g His career as a professional player started. ___

h His family received his Olympic medals. ___

Writing

1 Look at the Writing skills box.

Writing skills

Linkers

Use *although*, *but*, and *however* to link ideas.

I'm not good at judo, **but** I enjoy it.
Although I'm not good at judo, I enjoy it.
I'm not good at judo. **However**, I enjoy it.

2 Read the text. Circle the linkers *although*, *but*, and *however*.

Sports at my school
At school we play soccer and basketball, (but) we don't play hockey.
I love soccer. Although I'm good at kicking the ball, I'm not good at catching it. They don't choose me to play in goal.
I really like playing basketball. However, I'm not on the school team.

3 Fill in the chart with the information from the text.

play	soccer, basketball
don't play	
love	
good at	
not good at	
like	
problem	not on the school team

4 Now make notes about sports or other activities at your school.

5 Write about sports or other activities at your school. Use the text and your notes to help you.

Speaking

1 Listen and read.

2 Look at the Pronunciation box. Listen to the examples.

Pronunciation

/æ/ and /ʌ/ sounds

The letters *a* and *u* have different sounds.

/æ/	/ʌ/
cat	cut
mad	mud
track	truck

Listen again and repeat.

3 Listen and check (✓) the words that you hear.

1 bat   but
2 fan   fun
3 pack   puck
4 ran   run
5 hat   hut

4 Practice the dialog with your partner.

5 Change the words in blue. Write a new dialog. Now practice the dialog in class.

Review 11

Vocabulary
Sports equipment

1 Fill in the blanks with the words below.

> cap   fins   gloves   mask   puck   snorkel
> spikes   stick

1 You wear a _cap_ over your hair for swimming.
2 You wear _____ on your feet.
3 You wear a _____ over your eyes.
4 You use a _____ to help you breathe.
5 You wear _____ on your shoes to help you stay on the log.
6 You wear _____ on your hands.
7 You hit a _____ in a hockey game.
8 You hit the ball with a _____ .

Sports words

2 Correct the words.

> a court   goal posts   a racket   a referee

1 We need two ~~nets~~ for a rugby game. _goal posts_
2 I need a paddle to play tennis. _____
3 An umpire should watch our soccer game.
   _____
4 I reserved a field to play our tennis game.
   _____

Grammar
Indefinite pronouns

1 Fill in the blanks. Use indefinite pronouns.

1 I can hear a noise. Is there _anyone_ at the door?
2 There's _____ on the phone. I don't know who it is.
3 I'm hungry, but there isn't _____ in the refridgerator.
4 I've looked _____ for the car keys, but I can't find them.
5 Can you help me? There's _____ wrong with my computer.

Relative clauses

2 Write the sentences with relative clauses.

1 Underwater rugby is a sport. It's played in a pool.
   Underwater rugby is a sport which is
   played in a pool .
2 Alexander J. Cartwright was a man. He invented the rules of baseball. _____
   _____ .
3 New York is a city. Baseball started in New York.
   _____
   _____ .
4 William Morgan was an Amercan. He invented volleyball. _____
   _____ .
5 Hurley was a game. It was popular in Ireland in 1800. _____
   _____ .

Reading

> ### "Game Plan"
> The first football games were often disasters. There were no rules and there wasn't a referee to control the game. The teams didn't have any plans or strategies to win a game.
> In 1916, Cumberland was beaten 220–0 by Georgia Tech. It was a record score. After this embarrassing game, the coaches of the Cumberland team decided to do something. They began to watch the other teams playing games, and they made notes about their strengths and weaknesses. Then they planned a strategy to win – a "game plan".
> The technique was a great success. Other football teams started to copy their method. Soon business leaders were using "game plans" to sell their products, and to be better than their competitors.

1 Read the text and answer the questions.

1 What were the first football games like?
   disasters
2 Who created the "game plan"?
3 What did they do?
4 What did other football teams do?
5 What do business leaders use game plans for?

12 Imagine

Grammar: *would;* second conditional
Vocabulary: places; expressions with *take, make,* and *do*

Introducing the topic

Vocabulary

1 Match the pictures with the places below.

- [2] community center
- [ ] homeless shelter
- [ ] school campus
- [ ] gated community
- [ ] nursing home
- [ ] slum

🎧 **Now listen and repeat.**

Recycling

2 Where would you do these activities?

borrow a book ___library___

see a new movie _____

lift weights _____

buy some new clothes _____

watch a school play _____

eat lunch at school _____

Exploring the topic

THE TALK

THIS MONTH'S QUESTION:

WHAT WOULD YOU DO TO MAKE YOUR WORLD BETTER?

1 _At home_

My parents are really cool people, but they're both busy all the time. My mom works in a nursing home, and my dad's a lawyer. I'd like them to take more time off work. Then we could do more things as a family.

Mei-Li, Harbin, China

I'd have a place in our house where we could entertain our friends. When we want to play games like pool or table tennis, we go to the local community center. It's good there, but it would be better to stay home and have fun with our friends.

Pedro, Mexico City, Mexico

2 _____

I live in a very expensive neighborhood. It's a gated community, and there are guards when you come in. It's like a prison. I'd open up the neighborhood to others. Poorer families would enjoy the park and other things we have.

Antonia, Florida, U.S.A.

I do volunteer work at a homeless shelter. A lot of people in the shelter are great. I'd find a home for every one of them. They'd be really happy to have a place of their own.

Daryl, Toronto, Canada

3 _____

I go to a brand new school in a suburb. It's a great school, but there's one thing I'd definitely change. We have to stay on the school campus all day. I know they do it for safety reasons, but I'd find a better way to solve this problem. We're students, not prisoners!

Marty, Washington D.C., U.S.A.

I wouldn't change anything about my high school, except for one thing. We only have one room where the whole school can meet. Right now it's the lunchroom, gymnasium, and auditorium. I'd build a new gymnasium or auditorium.

Andi, San Juan, Puerto Rico

Reading

1 Read the text. Then write the headings in the correct place in the text.

At school
In the neighborhood
At home

2 🎧 Read and listen to the text. Write the correct name next to the sentences.

1 This person would like more freedom during school. ___*Marty*___

2 This person would like to share the neighborhood she lives in. _____

3 This person would like to enjoy more family time. _____

4 This person tries to help people who don't have homes. _____

5 This person would like more space at home. _____

6 This person would like more space at school. _____

Grammar

would

Talking about imaginary situations

1 Look at the chart.

Affirmative and negative
I'**d** (= I would) **clean up** the neighborhood.
I **wouldn't change** anything about my high school.

Questions
What would you **do** to make your world better?

2 Look at the pictures and the verbs in the box. What would you do in each situation?

> cut down   not learn   not swim   not use
> not touch   put away

1   I *wouldn't learn* to play the violin. It's difficult.

2   I _____ all the toys.

3   I _____ some of the trees.

4   I _____ touch the plate. It's hot.

5   I _____. There are sharks here.

3 Complete the conversation. Use the words in parentheses.

Petro: What (1) ___*would you do*___ (you / do)
with a million dollars?

Danila: Well, I (2) _____ (buy)
a new house for my family.

Petro: (3) _____ (you / get)
an expensive car too?

Danila: No, I (4) _____ (not buy) a car.
What about you? (5) _____
_____ (what / you / do)?

Petro: I (6) _____ (travel)
around the world.

Danila: Really? That's cool.

Finished?
Page 111, Puzzle 12A

Over to you!

4   **What would your ideal day be like? Make a list of things you would do, or not do! Tell the class.**

I wouldn't get up early. I'd have breakfast
in bed. I'd ...

Building the topic

Vocabulary

1 Match the pictures with the expressions below.

1 take part		do volunteer work	
make friends		make a living	
take exams		do exercise	

🎧 **Now listen and repeat.**

2 Read the text. Match the suggestions 1–3 to the responses A–C.

1 _B_   2 __   3 __

🎧 **Now listen and check.**

3 Can you think of one more expression for each of the verbs?

1 take _____

2 make _____

3 do _____

What would you do?

1 If people did more exercise, they'd be healthier.

2 If students got more practical training in school, it would be easier to make a living.

3 If more people did volunteer work, it would improve the lives of poor people.

Responses:

A I agree, but I think students should take exams too.

B I agree. If people joined a sports club, they'd also make new friends.

C I agree with you. If more people took part in volunteer programs, it would help a lot of people.

Grammar

Second conditional

Talking about imaginary situations and their results

1 Look at the chart.

if clause (simple past)	result clause (*would* + simple present)
If people **did** more exercise,	they**'d be** healthier.
If people **joined** a sports club,	they**'d make** new friends.

2 Match the two halves of the sentences.

1 If I lived in a cold country, _C_

2 If students did more homework, ___

3 If I had a lot of money, ___

4 If we went to Greece, ___

5 If factories reduced their pollution, ___

A they wouldn't have time to play sports.

B we'd see a lot of ancient buildings.

C I'd go skiing on the weekend.

D global warming would slow down.

E I'd buy an expensive house.

3 Fill in the blanks with the correct form of the verbs below.

> become   have   go   learn   live   rain

1 If you ___*became*___ a successful singer, you'd be rich.

2 If I _____ to college, I'd do a degree in politics.

3 If he _____ in New York, he'd have an apartment in Manhattan.

4 If I _____ to play an instrument, I'd choose the guitar.

5 If I _____ a computer, I'd send you an e-mail.

6 If it ____ in the desert, more plants and animals would live there.

4 Write sentences. Use the second conditional.

1 we recycle / there be less garbage

If we recycled, there *would be less garbage* .

2 she have the money / she buy the shoes

_____

_____

_____ .

3 she learn to drive / not take the bus

_____

_____

_____ .

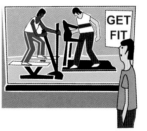

4 he do more exercise / he be stronger

_____

_____

_____ .

5 we drive less / we have cleaner air

_____

_____

_____ .

Finished?
Page 111, Puzzle 12B

Over to you!

5 Start a sentence with *If*. Can the class finish the sentence?

Student A: If I had more time, ...

Student B: I'd play soccer every day. If I ...

Living English

The AUCTION GAME

Instructions

Work in small groups.
There are ten correct, and ten incorrect sentences.
The aim of the game is to buy as many correct sentences as possible.
Each group has $5,000 to spend on correct sentences.
You have to spend $50 or more on a sentence.
Check (✓) the sentences you think are correct, and write how much you want to spend.
Your teacher will tell you which sentences are correct.
The group who has spent the most wins the sentence.
The winner of the game is the group which has bought the most correct sentences.

"What does Jannie like?" "She is tall, with short, red hair and freckles."

How big is your new television?

If I studied in England, my English would improve a lot.

I don't think Mireille will go to school in Canada.

If you study French, are you become a teacher?

His computer was taken from his office.

Damiano is allowed to stay out until ten every evening.

You're a good tennis player, don't you?

I lived in Singapore since 2003.

Joshua has never seen his favorite group in concert.

Shane's going to see his friends at the movie theater on Saturday.

I've yet told Cameron the news.

I'm worried about Tim and Karl. They might get lost on their hike.

She's the woman what coaches our women's soccer team.

How long did you worked in that factory?

There isn't somebody here who can help us.

Tasmin decided going to Japan and study there for a year.

I was riding my bike in the country when the storm started.

Soccer isn't as dangerous as ice hockey.

The red jacket in this shop is more expensiver than the blue one.

RESULT OF THE AUCTION
Check ten correct sentences.

Sentence	Correct sentence
1 ☐	
2 ☐	
3 ☐	
4 ☐	
5 ☐	
6 ☐	
7 ☐	
8 ☐	
9 ☐	
10 ☐	
11 ☐	
12 ☐	
13 ☐	
14 ☐	
15 ☐	
16 ☐	
17 ☐	
18 ☐	
19 ☐	
20 ☐	

Review 12

Vocabulary

Places

1 Write the names of the places.

1 A place where old people live. _nursing home_

2 A place for people who don't have a home.
   _____

3 A place where young people can meet friends and play games. _____

4 A place where poor people live. _____

5 A place where you see students. _____

6 A secure place for people who want to be safe.
   _____

Expressions with *take*, *make*, and *do*

2 Fill in the blanks with *take*, *make*, or *do* in the correct form.

Next summer, I'm going to (1) ____take____ part in a volunteer program in a poor village in Bolivia. There isn't much work, and it's hard for the people to (2) _____ a living.

There's only one small school, and the kids need help to (3) _____ exams. I'm going to (4) _____ volunteer work in the school. I'm also going to teach sports, and (5) _____ exercise like baseball, basketball and soccer.

I think I'll (5) _____ a lot of new friends!

Grammar

would

3 Fill in the blanks. Use *would* and the verbs in parentheses.

1 _Would you do_ volunteer work? (you / do)

2 I _____ shark diving. It's too dangerous. (not go)

3 What _____ for a special celebration? (your parents / do)

4 _____ in a gated community. (Danillo / not live)

5 I'd like to live in Tokyo for a year. _____ _____ Japanese there. (I / learn)

Second conditional

4 Fill in the blanks. Use the words in parentheses.

1 If they went to France for a year, they would ____learn____ (learn) French.

2 If Naomi _____ (enter) the competiton, she'd definitely win.

3 If they _____ (practice) more, their band would be really good.

4 If we left early in the morning, we _____ _____ (arrive) by lunchtime.

5 If more people _____ (do) volunteer work, it would make a big difference.

6 If you _____ (audition), you'd get the part.

Reading

1 Read the text. Fill in the blanks with the correct names.

WHAT WOULD YOU DO TO PROTECT THE ENVIRONMENT?

If I had the power, I'd make people use their cars for emergencies only. Sara

If I was rich, I'd give a lot of money to environmental groups, and I wouldn't have a big house or a big car. Pablo

If I was a celebrity, I'd speak out about the environment. I think celebs really care about it. Naomi

If I had the chance, I'd work in the Amazon rainforest. I'd try to improve the situation there. I'm planning to study Environmental Sciences at college. Fran

I'd make factories find new ways to produce goods, and I'd make everything recyclable. I'd also make businesses pay a lot of money if they created too much pollution. Jeff

1 _____ thinks celebrities really worry about the environment.

2 _____ would make companies pay for producing too much pollution.

3 _____ would drive a small car.

4 _____ wouldn't use her car all the time.

5 _____ is interested in planting trees to help the environment.

puzzle 1a

Find eight adjectives in the wordsearch

C	V	H	Z	K	L	W	P	Q	T
F	H	T	E	N	M	U	P	N	D
J	U	I	I	L	S	L	E	A	A
X	Z	N	Q	H	P	D	L	B	R
O	A	A	Y	I	I	F	A	F	I
A	U	Q	L	F	S	V	U	Z	N
F	I	T	N	I	H	S	P	L	G
K	K	O	C	A	Y	Q	I	N	L
N	C	A	R	R	O	G	A	N	T
I	O	F	Y	L	P	D	B	O	H

puzzle 1b

Who is who? Write the names.
Luke isn't wearing a red and white shirt. Davide doesn't have blond hair. Julio isn't wearing a striped shirt. Arturo isn't wearing a plain white shirt. Davide isn't wearing a patterned shirt.

Julio

puzzle 2a

Use the orange letters to find out what Taylor has done.

Taylor Jackman has never forgotten an appointment. He has never told a lie. He has never read someone else's e-mail or cheated on a test. He has never chewed second-hand gum either! Is Taylor perfect? Not really, because he has

p _ _ _ _ _ d _ _ r _ _ _ _ _ _ _ _ l
_ _ k _ _ on his friends.

puzzle 3a

Sharon is going on a trip. Complete the expressions about the things she's going to do. Then use the circled letters to find out where she's going to go.

○ _ _ ○ _ for a passport
book her _ _ _ _ _ _ ○ _
pack her _ _ _ ○ _ _
_ _ _ _ ○ a taxi to the airport

She is going to visit _ _ _ _ _ _ _ .

puzzle 2b

Ken didn't know what to do with his life: go to college, get a job, travel around the world? He's thought and thought about it. Use the clues to find out what he's done.

The first three letters of the twelfth month of the year. _ _ _
Two people are, but one person _ _.
Another name for "me" is _.
You can turn the TV off or _ _.
Ken has made a _ _ _ _ _ _ _ _ _ _.

puzzle 3b

Joni is going on vacation, and is very worried. What's she thinking?

LOT MET THIS GIG
I MIGHT *GET* *LOST* .

A ED FRIGHTENS INK IT MOM
_ _ _ _ _ _ _ _ _ NOT _ _ _ _ _ _
_ _ _ _ _ _ .

BEDTIME RUG HI
_ _ _ _ _ _ _ _ _ _ _ _ _ _ .

① Read the website advertisement. Match the headings to the paragraphs.

② Think of an evening class you would like to advertise. For example, salsa classes, kick boxing classes, yoga classes. Find out some information about the things you learn in the classes.

③ Make notes for each of the headings below. Find pictures to go with your notes.

④ Design the advertisement for your class. Present the advertisement to your class.

Back | Stop ✖ | Home 🏠 | Favourites 📄 | History | Print 🖨

Address | www.thekungfuclubaustin.wwb | Go

KUNG FU CLUB
TEACHING KUNG FU AND TAI CHI SINCE 1983

1 **Time of classes and contact details**
2 **Other information**
3 **Our program**
4 **We welcome all new students**
5 **Why come to our club?**

A _____

We train small groups in traditional Chinese Kung Fu and Tai Chi Chuan.
We also teach the history, language and cultural traditions of martial arts.

B _____

The classes are for adults and children of all ages and fitness levels,
from beginner to advanced.

C _____

Students develop their confidence and concentration, self-defense,
control and respect.

D _____

We also organize competitions, training camps, dinners, and other events.

E _____

Autumn schedule
Monday–Friday, 7.30 pm–9.00 pm.

Call now for more information.
You won't be sorry!

The Kung Fu Club, Austin
e-mail: admission.thekungfuclub@austincr
website: www.thekungfuclubaustin.wwb

engage

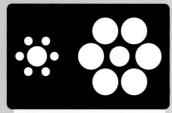

magazine two

puzzle 4a

What was happening to Wendy?
Unscramble the letters.

IGH WA TMA AVI
RE. S H A N SHE NG

SHE _____ .

puzzle 4b

Unscramble the words. What was Rob doing
at 3 p.m.? Use the orange letters.

LNGIAWK W A L K I N G
MISNIWMG □□□□□□□
GADRIEN □□□□□□□
NELIGPES □□□□□□□□

He was □□o□Bo□□□□□□□ .

puzzle 5a

Optical illusions

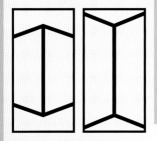

Which of the center
lines is longer?

Which central
circle is bigger?

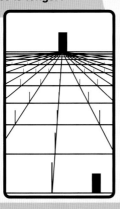

Which rectangle is smaller?

Who's taller?

puzzle 5b

Test your knowledge of the animal world
with our quiz.

Superlative animals

1   The largest animal in the world is the blue whale.
    How long is it?
    a 34 meters   b 60 meters   c 100 meters

2   The fastest land animal is the cheetah. It can go:
    a 93 km/h   b 113 km/ h   c 123 km/h

3   One of the most dangerous spiders is the
    Funnel-web spider. It comes from…
    a Africa   b Asia   c Australia

puzzle 6b

Use the orange letters from the sentences to find
out what Lucy Maddison has done in Africa. You
can only use the letters once.

LUCY MADISON WAS BORN IN 1982.
SHE'S APPEARED IN CONCERTS WITH
FAMOUS GROUPS.

She's   r ○○○○○○ ○○○○○
and ○○○○○ p ○○ g ○○○
for poor people in Africa.

puzzle 6a

BREAK THE CODE and find the name of the product.

A	C	D	E	G	I	L	N	O	P	R	S	T	U
●	◇		□							♣		○	

First, we ◇♣□●○□ the product.
Next, we ✚□△?♥≋ the product.
Then, we 8♣✕✚✔◇□. Finally, we △□☆☆ it!
What's the name of our product? ◇✕✕☆ ✚✔✚□ ◇✚△ !

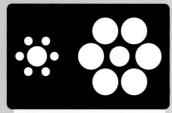

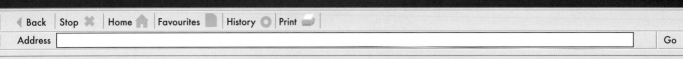

◀ Back | Stop ✖ | Home 🏠 | Favourites ▮ | History ◯ | Print ⊿

Address [   ] | Go

Youth Action

A website written by young people for young people.

Your news, views, and reviews from the neighborhood.

Join now

1 Read the text about a website. Which paragraph talks about each of the following?

_B_ What's on the website.

___ What you can discuss on the website.

___ Who organizes the website.

___ General information about the purpose of the site.

___ A prize that the website has won.

2 Think about a new website for your school or neighborhood. Invent a name for the website. Make notes for each of the headings above, and write a welcome message.

3 Find or take pictures to go with your notes.

4 Design a homepage for your website.

A Youth Action provides young people in the neighborhood with information, advice and support. It also gives you an opportunity to write about things that are important to you, and gives you a chance to meet other people online.

B On the site, you can read CD and movie reviews, and find out about youth events in your neighborhood. You can also post your photos in the Youth Action Picture log via your mobile phone.

C You can also talk about your problems and get professional help. And you can use the chat forum to talk about school, college, jobs, health problems, bullying, crime, and other things!

D Six young people are in charge of the website, and they decide what is going to be on the website. There are also another 30 writers, and 10 young people who control the web forum. To become a member of the writer's club, click on "join now".

E In 2007, we won the Youth Website of the Year Award, for our achievement in helping young people in the neighborhood.

puzzle 7a

What are the objects?
Clue: you need them on vacation!

puzzle 7b

Put S (Strict) or NS (Not Strict) for these rules.

CRAZY RULES

1 My mom lets me borrow her car. ___

2 My mom makes me clean her car. ___

3 My dad doesn't make me do my homework. ___

4 I'm allowed to go to dance clubs. ___

5 My mom makes me stay out late. ___

6 My dad doesn't let me wear makeup. ___

7 I'm not allowed to wash the dishes. ___

puzzle 8a

Unscramble the names to complete the predictions.

l **Chad Hilveren** says: "I'm sure I'll _ _ _ _ _ _ _ _ _ _ _ _. I'll be a great father."

2 **Gerta Merid** says: "I'll probably _ _ _ _ _ _ _ _ _ _ before I'm 25."

3 **Pennie Obussas** says: "I definitely won't _ _ _ _ _ _ _ _ _ _ _ _ _. It's too risky."

4 **Greta Adu** says: "I'll probably _ _ _ _ _ _ _ _ _ from college in 2009."

5 **Paola J. Profby** says: "I'll probably _ _ _ _ _ _ _ _ _ _ _ _ _ _ when I finish high school."

puzzle 8b Find the words.

population
global warming
fossil fuel
rain forest
extinct
alternative energy

W	P	Y	B	L	Y	E	T	M	A
F	O	S	S	I	L	F	U	E	L
S	P	I	R	J	C	R	V	X	T
V	U	F	R	W	U	V	D	T	E
G	L	O	B	A	L	U	C	I	R
D	A	R	C	R	I	Y	X	N	N
O	T	E	P	M	U	N	H	C	A
S	I	S	T	I	D	E	J	T	T
A	O	T	E	N	E	R	G	Y	I
B	N	F	U	G	L	A	K	J	V
E	D	G	K	J	P	I	B	D	E

puzzle 9a

There is something wrong with this story. Can you fix it? Change the words in CAPITAL LETTERS.

AUDIENCE • AUDITION • CONTESTANT JUDGES • HOST • PRIZES

1 Annie Belfer wanted to be a RECORDING CONTRACT in a TV talent contest.

2 She went to an AUDIENCE in her home town.

3 She sang her song for the four PRIZES, who were all famous people.

4 She was very excited about the JUDGES: a car and a lot of money.

5 During the first show, the AUDITION announced her name.

6 She went on stage, saw the huge CONTESTANT, and was so scared by all the people that she couldn't sing!

puzzle 9b

Test your music knowledge with our quiz.

① **Cry Me A River** was sung by:
a Justin Timberlake   b Robbie Williams.

② The album **Dangerously in Love** was recorded by:
a Britney Spears   b Beyoncé.

③ Avril Lavigne's hit **Knocking on Heaven's Door** was originally recorded by:
a Bob Dylan   b Elvis Presley.

④ **Harry Potter** was written by:
a J.R.R. Tolkien   b J.K.Rowling.

⑤ **Lord of the Rings** was directed by:
a Steven Spielberg   b Peter Jackson.

⑥ **Where is the Love?** was performed by:
a No Doubt   b The Black Eyed Peas.

1 Read the tips on traveling in South Africa. Match the headings with the paragraphs.

Eating out   Health   Stay safe
Think before you pack   Traveling around

Cape Town

South Africa:
top travel tips for a good trip

4 _____
Crime is the same as the rest of the world. It isn't a good idea to carry too much money or wear jewelry or expensive watches. If you carry lots of cameras and walk around with maps, you'll look like a tourist, and you'll be a target for robbers. Lock your door at night and avoid some areas in the city when it gets dark.

Cape Malay food

1 _____
You don't need a heavy bag. Take light clothes. A hat and a cotton scarf might be useful, and bring your sunglasses. The African sun is very bright. The sun is also very strong and you need to use a good sunblock. However, South Africa isn't always warm. It gets cold, especially on winter evenings. Bring a warm jacket, a jersey, socks, good walking shoes, and a rain jacket with you too. It can be warm and sunny in Cape Town, but it can be cold and very windy at the top of Table Mountain.

2 _____
You don't need a yellow fever vaccination in South Africa. You also don't need to take malaria tablets in many of the tourist areas. There's malaria in north and east of the country in the summer months. You need to take tablets here. Always use insect spray, wear long pants, shoes, and long-sleeved shirts at night.

3 _____
You aren't allowed to drive without an international driver's license in South Africa. Always carry the license with you. Watch out for animals in the country, like dogs, cows and antelope, especially at night. Drive slowly, and drive on the left.

5 _____
South African food is multi-cultural. You can find traditional Dutch sausages, English meat pies, dishes from India, Indonesia, and China (Cape Malay food). The food is delicious. There are also restaurants where native African food is served. In some restaurants crocodile steak and antelope meat are offered.

Enjoy your trip!

Springbok antelope

2 You're going to write some travel tips for people visiting your country. Think about the advice you think they will need. Make notes for each of the headings above.

3 Find or take pictures to go with your notes.

4 Write your travel tips for your country. Then present your tips to the class.

puzzle 10a

What is Tom's relationship to Harry?

Harry fell in love with Tom's sister Rose. But they broke up and Rose got married to Harry's brother Jim. Tom broke up with his girlfriend Megan, and made up with his ex-girlfriend, Anne, Harry's sister. Anne and Tom got married.

Tom is Harry's

_ _ _ _ _ _ _ _ - _ _ - _ _ _ .

puzzle 10b

What's Jon going to do tonight? Use the letters in the circles to complete the sentence.

Jon Ⓒ A N ' T S T A N Ⓓ staying in.
Although he doesn't _ _ _ Ⓓ playing computer games.
He has _ _ _ _ _ _ _ _ Ⓓ to go to a party tonight.
He has also _ _ _ _ _ _ Ⓞ _ _ _ D to go to a concert.
His friend _ Ⓞ _ _ S inviting him to the movies.
Jon is _ _ _ _ _ _ _ _ _ _ Ⓞ in playing soccer.

Jon has D _ _ _ _ _ _ D to go out with his girlfriend.

puzzle 11a

What are the objects?

1 _ _ _ _ _ 2 _ _ _ _ _ 3 _ _ _ _ _ _ _ _
4 _ _ _ _ _ 5 _ _ _ _ _ 6 _ _ _ _ _ _ _ _

puzzle 11b

Complete the crossword.

Across

2 It's a place where you can learn about history.

4 It's something that you need to breathe underwater.

5 It's something that you need when it's hot.

6 It's a place where you can borrow books.

Down

1 It's someone who enters a competition.

3 It's someone who fixes cars.

puzzle 12a

Where does Kenji live?

He doesn't live in a
G _ _ D C _ _ _ _ _ Y

He doesn't live in a
H _ _ _ _ _ S S _ _ _ _ R

He doesn't live in a
S _ M

He lives in a
N _ _ _ _ G H _ E

puzzle 12b

Find the expressions.

DPPOZVOEFLUNLTKEEXRWLOXSRK

FTDPOLHQEOMZEAQWLOHRK

CTAYKUETEDXANMS

OMAKYEBALJEIVWINSG

PGQEOBAUJKNGEREJLSUMSPQLISNMG

MYAORKEAHSMCILASTWAPKE

1 Read the proposal for a new soap opera. How many characters does it describe? What are the characters talking about?

Darkness and Light

This is a story that takes place in a very rich neighborhood outside of New York City. It's about four large families who live near each other. They hang out together, they have parties at each other's houses, they date and break up with each other. However, two of the families, the Peters and the Morrisons, are enemies. They hate each other and they have had problems for many years.

Sample script

[Magda Darlington is in her 50s. She's married to her third husband, John Peters. Amanda Peters is her step-daughter. She's eighteen years old. Jason is nineteen. He's the son of their neighbors and enemies, the Morrisons.]

Magda: I won't tell you again - you can't marry Jason Morrison.
Amanda: Why not?
Magda: You know you can't marry anyone from that family.
Jason: What do you mean, that family? There's nothing wrong with my family!
Magda: Be quiet! Amanda. Now, don't lie to me. Would you agree to marry him if he asked you?
Amanda: Yes, I would. And you can't tell me what I can do. You aren't my mother.
Jason [holding Amanda's arm]: Anyway, it's my decision. I know she'll marry me - because she won't have any choice. I'm taking her away with me right now.
Amanda: Jason! What do you think you're doing?
Magda: Come back here!
Peter [entering room]: What's going on here? Amanda? Jason?
Madga: Jason is taking your daughter away. You have to do something! She doesn't love him, and I know he isn't in love with her. DO something!
[Peter holds Jason's arm and there's a scream. It isn't clear what's happened. Fade out...]

2 Invent four characters for a new soap, and think about the relationships between them.

3 Decide on a scene for the soap. Make notes on a story for that scene.

4 Write a brief description of the show, the main characters and the storyline. Then write a short script using the four characters. Present it to the class.

Grammar summary

Unit 1

be like / look like

Personality	
What **is** she **like**?	She's arrogant and pushy.
Appearance	
What **does** she **look like**?	She's tall. She has long, wavy hair.

We use *What ... like?* to ask about ... personality.
What are they like? They're friendly and fun.
We use *What do/does ... look like?* to ask about appearance.
What does he look like? He's tall, handsome, and he has dark hair.

How + adjective, / be made of / be like

How + adjective	
How long are the skirts**?**	They're very long.
What ... made of?	
What's it **made of**?	It's made of wood.
What ... like?	
What's your board like?	It's blue and green.

We use *How* + adjective to ask about age, size, height, weight, length, speed, etc, of things.
How fast is it? It's very fast. It can travel 150 kilometers per hour.
We use *What's it like?* to ask about the appearance of things.
What are Goth clothes like?
They're mostly black.
We use *What's it made of?* to ask about materials.
What are they made of?
They're made of metal and leather.

Unit 2

Present perfect (*ever / never*)

Questions	Answers
Have I / you / we / they **ever cheated** on a test?	
Has he / she **ever read** a friend's e-mail.	Yes, I **have**. / No, I **haven't**.
Negative statements	
I **have never cheated** on a test.	
He **has never read** a friend's e-mail.	

We form the present perfect with *Have / has* and a past participle.
Have you ever told a lie to a friend?
We use present perfect questions with *ever* to ask about life experiences.
Have you ever forgotten a date or an appointment?
We use *never* to form negative statements about life experiences.
I've never written a fan letter to a celebrity.

Present perfect (*just / already / yet*)

Affirmative	Negative
I**'ve already visited** three universities.	
A local bookstore **has just made** a donation.	I **haven't made** a decision **yet**.
Questions	**Answers**
Have you **visited** your favorite colleges **yet**?	Yes, I have. / No, I haven't.

We use the present perfect with *just*, *already*, and *yet* to talk about recent news and events.
We use *just* in affirmative sentences to talk about very recent news.
They've just made a big announcement.
We use *yet* in questions and negative sentences to talk about news and events happening up to now.
Have you signed up to help with the Spring Dance yet? We haven't chosen a theme yet.
We use *already* in affirmative sentences to talk about news and events that happened before now.
He's already visited his favorite college.

Unit 3

going to and will

Plan	Offer
I'm going to apply for my passport.	I'll help you.
I'm not going to see you for three months.	We'll come to the airport to say goodbye.

We use *going to* to talk about plans.
We form *going to* sentences with subject + *be* + *going to* + infinitive.
I'm going to book my flight to Tokyo next week.
I'm not going to see you for three months.
We use *will* to make offers.
We form *will* sentences with subject + *will* + infinitive.
I'll pick you up from the airport.

might

Affirmative	Negative
I might get lost.	I might not fit in.

We use *might* to talk about future possibilities.
We form affirmative sentences with subject + *might* + infinitive.
I might be rude.
We form negative sentences with subject + *might not* + infinitive.
I might not understand.

Unit 4

Past progressive and simple past

Describing the scene – past progressive	
Affirmative	Negative
He was sleeping.	He wasn't working.
They were dancing.	They weren't singing.
Describing a sequence of events – simple past	
He fell asleep. He heard some music, he wrote 'Yesterday'.	

We use the past progressive to describe scenes in the past.
We form the past progressive (affirmative) with subject + *was / were* + *-ing* form.
Some men were dancing around him.
Her hair wasn't growing.
We use the simple past to describe a sequence of events in the past.
Then, she woke up. She decided to experiment with different mixtures form Africa. One of the mixtures worked.

Regular verbs end in *-ed.*
work → worked
decide → decided
try → tried
Irregular verbs in the simple past don't follow a pattern. See the irregular verb list on page 118 and try to learn them.

Past progressive and simple past (when)

Past progressive	+ when +	simple past
He was walking his dog		it got covered with sticky seeds
He was stirring a soda drink outside	when	it became very cold.
He was singing at church		he suddenly had an idea.

We use past progressive and simple past with *when* to talk about an interrupted action in the past.
Frank was coming out of his house when he saw his drink.

Unit 5

Comparative adjectives

Short comparative adjectives			
Soccer is	slower	than	rugby.
Soccer rules are	easier	than	rugby rules.
We play rugby in a	bigger field	than	football.
Soccer is	nicer	than	football.
Long comparative adjectives			
Rugby is	more exciting	than	football.
Rugby and football are	more dangerous	than	soccer.

We use comparatives to talk about differences between two things or people.
Some short adjectives form comparatives with *-er* or *-r:*
fast → faster   nice → nicer
For adjectives ending in *-y*, we change *y* to *i:*
easy → easier
For adjectives ending in one vowel and one consonant, we double the consonant:
big → bigger
For long adjectives, we form comparatives with *more* + adjective + *than.*
interesting → more interesting

(*not*) *as ... as*

(*not*) *as ... as*
Rugby is **as competitive as** football
Rugby is **not as rough as** football.

We use *as ... as* to talk about similarities.
Soccer is as challenging as rugby.
We use *not as ... as* to talk about differences.
Soccer isn't as expensive as football.

Superlative adjectives

Superlative adjectives
A Syrian hymn is **the** old**est** song in the world.
It is one of **the most popular** music festivals in the U.K.

We use superlative adjectives to say that one thing is different from everything else.
It's the largest instrument in the world.
Some short adjectives form the superlative with adjective + *-est*.
old → *the oldest*
For adjectives ending in *-y*, we change *y* to *i*:
easy → *the easiest*
For adjectives ending in one vowel and one consonant, we double the consonant:
big → *biggest*
For long adjectives, we form the superlative with *the most* + adjective.
interesting → *the most interesting*

Unit 6

Present perfect (*for / since*)

Chocolate Farm **has been** in business	**for**	nine years.
Elise and Evan **have had** their company	**since**	1998.

We use the present perfect to talk about present activities that started in the past.
They have had their company since 1998.
We use *for* to talk about the period of time up to the present. For example, *for twelve years, for three months, for two days.*
Elise has made chocolate for more than fifteen years.
We use *since* to talk about the time when an activity started. For example, *since 1995, since last year, since she was ten years old.*
He's designed websites since he was twelve.

Present perfect and simple past

Present Perfect	Simple past
Bono **has written** music for several movies. (we don't say when)	He **married** Ali in 1982. (we say when)

We can use present perfect to talk about personal achievements in the past. We don't say when they happened.
He's met politicians and leaders from around the world.
We can use the simple past to talk about personal achievements in the past. We say when they happened.
He joined U2 in 1976.

Unit 7

Question tags

Question tags with *be*	
Positive statement + negative tag	Negative statement + affirmative tag
It's cold, **isn't it**?	**It isn't** cold, **is it**?
Islanders are friendly, **aren't they**?	**There aren't** any dress rules, **are there**?

Watch this: **I'm** late, **aren't I**?

We use question tags to check information.
There aren't any rules, are there?
We put a negative tag after affirmative statement. The answer is normally *yes*.
It's hot, isn't it? Yes, it is.
We put an affirmative tag after negative statements. The answer is normally *no*.
It isn't hot, is it? No, it isn't.
Statements with *be* have question tags with *be*.
The question tag for *I am* is *aren't I*.
I'm sunburnt, aren't I?

Question tags with *do*	
Positive statement + negative tag	Negative statement + affirmative tag
It **rains** a lot, **doesn't it**?	She **doesn't need** a vaccine, **does she**?
Most people **speak** English, **don't they**?	We **don't need** a driver's licence, **do we**?

Statements with the present simple have question tags with *do / does*.
She doesn't need a yellow fever vaccination, does she?

Grammar summary

make / let / be allowed

Obligation
The school **makes** children want to learn.
Teachers **don't make** students go to classes.

Permission
The school **lets** students decide rules for on bedtimes.
The school **doesn't let** students stay up after 10:30.
Students **are allowed** to have a lot of freedom.
They **aren't allowed** to play the drums at 4 a.m.

We can talk about obligations with *make* + object + infinitive.

The teachers make us do our homework.
My parents don't make me do the shopping.

We can use *let* and *be allowed to* to talk about permission.

We use *let* + object + infinitive.

The teachers let the students do what they like with their own free time.
My parents don't let me play music late at night.

We use *be allowed* + infinitive (with *to*).

Students are allowed to make decisions.
Students aren't allowed to break this rule.

Unit 8

will / won't

Affirmative	Negative
I**'ll probably / definitely study** English.	I **probably / definitely won't stay** in New York.

We use *will / won't* to make predictions about the future.

I think a lot more people will visit our country in the next ten years.

We can use the adverbs *probably* and *definitely* with *will*.

I'll probably get a job in a hotel.

In affirmative sentences, *probably* and *definitely* go after *will*.

I'll definitely go to a good university.

In negative sentences, *probably* and *definitely* go before *won't*.

I probably won't study in another country.

First conditional

If clause (simple present)	Result clause (*will* + infinitive)
Affirmative	
If we **throw away** all our household waste,	we**'ll create** a lot of pollution.
Negative	
If we **grow** plants that do well in hot, dry countries,	we **won't run out of** food.

We use the first conditional to talk about possible events and their results.

If we stop cutting down trees, a lot of plants and animals will survive.

We form the *if* clause with the simple present. We form the result clause with *will / won't* + infinitive.

If we save energy, global warming will slow down.
If we develop alternative energy, we won't need fossil fuel.

Unit 9

Passive (simple present)

Passive (simple present)
One contestant **is sent** home.
Auditions **are organized**.
The singers **aren't chosen** by the judges.
The finale **isn't held** in a TV studio.

We use the passive in the simple present to talk about processes and procedures.

We form the passive (simple present) with subject + *be* + past participle.

The final isn't held in the TV studio, it's held in a big theater.

Passive (simple past)

Passive (simple past)
He **was sent** to ballet school.
He **wasn't bullied** by the other kids.
Other young dancers **were inspired** by his story.

We use the passive in the simple past to talk about events and processes in the past.

We form the passive (simple past) with subject + *was / were* + past participle.

He was awarded the prize.
They weren't bullied at school.

Unit 10
Verbs + prepositions

Affirmative and negative			
Tina	**got married**	to	her boyfriend.
She	didn't **make up**	with	Katie.

Many verbs need a preposition before the object.
Heidi got married to Peter.
Zeke fell in love with Maria.

Questions
Who will Clarissa live **with**?
Who will Tanisha get married **to**?

In questions, the preposition goes at the end.
Who will Maria fall in love with?

Infinitive or -ing

Verb + *to* + infinitive	
decide	**I decided to stay** in my home town.
arrange	I've **arranged to go** to a party.
promise	You **promised to work** hard.

Verb + -ing	
can't stand	They **can't stand seeing** me with this guy.
keep	My parents **keep asking** me to stay.
mind	I **don't mind living** on my own.
not interested in	I'm **not interested in going** to classes I hate.

Unit 11
Indefinite pronouns

some - affirmative statements
Someone in my class does this sport.
You have to wear **something** on your feet.
This sport takes place **somewhere** in the U.K.

any - negative and questions
You don't need **anything** else.
Does **anyone** know?
Is there **anywhere** you can play this sport in South America?

every - Affirmative statements
This is a sport for **everyone**.
Everything ends up dirty.
These are clubs **everywhere** in the U.S.

We use *something*, *someone*, and *somewhere* with affirmative sentences.
They throw something at the other person.
We use *anything*, *anyone*, and *anywhere* with negative sentences and questions.
You don't need anything.

Has anyone ever played underwater rugby?
We use *every* in affirmative sentences to mean all the things, all the people and all the places.
Everything is wet.
We use a singular verb with indefinite pronouns.
Everyone enjoys this sport.

Relative clauses

who
William Webb Ellis was a person. He invented rugby.
William Webb Ellis was the **person who** invented rugby.

which / that
Tennis is a sport. It's popular all over the world.
Tennis is **a sport that** is popular all over the world.
They used the ball. It was made from part of an animal.
The ball which they used was made from part of an animal.

where
France is a country. Tennis originated in France.
France was **the place where** tennis originated.

We use relative clauses to identify people, things or places.
We use *who* for people.
Monks were the people who first played tennis.
We use *which / that* for things.
A paddle was the equipment that people first used to hit the ball.
Tennis is a sport which you play with a racket.
We use *where* for places.
England was the country where the game started.

Unit 12

would

Affirmative and negative
I**'d clean up** the neighborhood.
I **wouldn't change** anything about it.

Questions
What would you **do** to make your world better?

We use *would* to talk about possibilities. The short form of *would* is *'d*.
We form affirmative sentences with subject + *would* + infinitive.
I'd open up the neighborhood to others.
We form negative sentences with subject + *would* + *not* + infinitive.
I wouldn't live in a gated community.
We form questions with *would* + subject + infinitive.
What would you do to improve your school?

Grammar summary

Second conditional

If clause (simple past)	result clause (would + simple present)
Affirmative	
If people **joined** a sports club, they **would make** new friends.	
Negative	
If they **gave** more tickets,	**a lot of people wouldn't pay** them.

We use the second conditional to talk about possible situations and their results or consequences.

If people did more voluntary work, it would make a lot of difference.

We form the *if* clause with the simple past. We form the result clause with *would / wouldn't* + infinitive.

If students took fewer exams, they'd have more time.

If we learnt more languages, it wouldn't help with the world's problems.

Irregular verbs

babysit	babysat	babysat
be	was/were	been
become	became	become
begin	began	begun
break	broke	broken
build	built	built
buy	bought	bought
catch	caught	caught
choose	chose	chosen
come	came	come
cut	cut	cut
do	did	done
draw	drew	drawn
dream	dreamt	dreamt
drink	drank	drunk
drive	drove	driven
eat	ate	eaten
fall	fell	fallen
feel	felt	felt
fight	fought	fought
find	found	found
forget	forgot	forgotten
fly	flew	flown
freeze	froze	frozen
get	got	gotten
give	gave	given
go	went	been (gone)
grow	grew	grown
have	has/have	had
hear	heard	heard
hide	hid	hidden
hit	hit	hit
hold	held	held
hurt	hurt	hurt
know	knew	known
leave	left	left
lose	lost	lost
make	made	made
meet	met	met
put	put	put
read	read	read
ride	rode	ridden
run	ran	run
see	saw	seen
sell	sold	sold
send	sent	sent
set	set	set
sing	sang	sung
sink	sank	sunk
sit	sat	sat
sleep	slept	slept
speak	spoke	spoken
spill	spilt	spilt
stand	stood	stood
steal	stole	stolen
stick	stuck	stuck
swim	swam	swum
take	took	taken
teach	taught	taught
tear	tore	torn
tell	told	told
think	thought	thought
throw	threw	thrown
wake	woke	woken
wear	wore	worn
win	won	won
write	wrote	written

Word list

Remember this?

Travel activities
buy souvenirs /ˌbaɪ ˌsuvəˈnɪrz/
buy a ticket /ˌbaɪ ə ˈtɪkɪt/
carry your passport /ˌkæri yər ˈpæspɔrt/
drop litter /ˌdrɑp ˈlɪt̬ər/
take a tour /ˌteɪk ə ˈtʊr/
use a credit card /ˌyuz ə ˈkrɛdət ˌkɑrd/

Health problems
cold /koʊld/
headache /ˈhɛdeɪk/
sore throat /ˌsɔr ˈθroʊt/
sprained ankle /ˌspreɪnd ˈæŋkl/
sunburn /ˈsʌnbərn/
toothache /ˈtuθeɪk/

Unit 1

Personality
arrogant /ˈærəgənt/
confident /ˈkɑnfədənt/
daring /ˈdɛrɪŋ/
fit /fɪt/
fun /fʌn/
helpful /ˈhɛlpfl/
pushy /ˈpʊʃi/
shy /ʃaɪ/

Materials and patterns
cotton /ˈkɑtn/
leather /ˈlɛðər/
metal /ˈmɛt̬l/
patterned /ˈpæt̬ərnd/
plain /pleɪn/
plastic /ˈplæstɪk/
striped /straɪpt/
wood /wʊd/
wool /wʊl/

Living English
director /dəˈrɛktər, daɪ-/
editor /ˈɛdət̬ər/
film producer /ˈfɪlm prəˌdusər/

Review 1
design /dɪˈzaɪn/
loose /lus/

Unit 2

Bad habits
cheat on a test /ˌtʃit ɑn ə ˈtɛst/
chew gum /ˌtʃu ˈgʌm/

fall in love /ˌfɔl ɪn ˈlʌv/
forget an appointment /fərˌgɛt ən əˈpɔɪntmənt/
play a practical joke /ˌpleɪ ə ˌpræktɪkl ˈdʒoʊk/
read someone's e-mail /ˌrid ˌsʌmwʌnz ˈimeɪl/
tell a lie /ˌtɛl ə ˈlaɪ/
write a fan letter /ˌraɪt ə ˈfæn ˌlɛt̬ər/

Expressions with make
make a change /ˌmeɪk ə ˈtʃeɪndʒ/
make a decision /ˌmeɪk ə dɪˈsɪʒn/
make a donation /ˌmeɪk ə doʊˈneɪʃn/
make a mistake /ˌmeɪk ə mɪˈsteɪk/
make a plan /ˌmeɪk ə ˈplæn/
make a suggestion /ˌmeɪk ə səgˈdʒɛstʃn/
make an announcement /ˌmeɪk ən əˈnaʊnsmənt/

Living English
announce /əˈnaʊns/
alligator /ˈæləgeɪt̬ər/
astrophysics /ˈæstroʊˌfɪzɪks/
homeless reptiles /ˌhoʊmləs ˈrɛptaɪlz/
pet /pɛt/
tortoise /ˈtɔrt̬əs/

Review 2
white lies /ˌwaɪt ˈlaɪz/

Unit 3

Travel expressions
apply for a passport /əˌplaɪ fər ə ˈpæspɔrt/
book a flight /ˌbʊk ə ˈflaɪt/
pack your bags /ˌpæk yər ˈbægz/
pick someone up /ˌpɪk sʌmwʌn ˈʌp/
see someone off /ˌsi sʌmwʌn ˈɔf/
take a taxi /ˌteɪk ə ˈtæksi/

Living overseas
be homesick for /ˌbi ˈhoʊmsɪk fər/
be rude /ˌbi ˈrud/
get lost /ˌgɛt ˈlɑst/
make friends with /ˌmeɪk ˈfrɛndz wɪð/

not fit in /ˌnɑt ˌfɪt ˈɪn/
not get along with /ˌnɑt ˌgɛt əˈlɑŋ wɪð/
not understand /ˌnɑt ˌʌndərˈstænd/

Living English
exchange student /ɪksˈtʃeɪndʒ ˌstudnt/
independent /ˌɪndɪˈpɛndənt/
informal /ɪnˈfɔrml/
long-sleeved shirt /ˌlɑŋ ˌslivd ˈʃərt/
patient /ˈpeɪʃnt/
understanding /ˌʌndərˈstændɪŋ/

Magazine 1
control /kənˈtroʊl/
concentration /ˌkɑnsənˈtreɪʃn/
develop /dɪˈvɛləp/
fitness /ˈfɪtnəs/
self-defense /ˌsɛlf dɪˈfɛns/

Unit 4

Sleeping and dreaming
daydream /ˈdeɪdrim/
dream /drim/
fall asleep /ˌfɔl əˈslip/
have nightmares /ˌhæv ˈnaɪtmɛrz/
wake up /ˌweɪk ˈʌp/
yawn /yɔn/

Making things
add /æd/
freeze /friz/
press /prɛs/
remove /rɪˈmuv/
separate /ˈsɛpəreɪt/
stick /stɪk/
stir /stɔr/
tear /tɛr/

Living English
insecure /ˌɪnsəˈkyʊr/
panic /ˈpænɪk/
recurring dreams /rɪˌkərɪŋ ˈdrimz/
support /səˈpɔrt/
sweaty /ˈswɛt̬i/
out of breath /ˌaʊt̬ əv ˈbrɛθ/

Review 4
admire /ədˈmaɪər/
chauffeur /ˈʃoʊfər/
pretend /prɪˈtɛnd/
simple /ˈsɪmpl/

Unit 5

Describing sports
competitive /kəmˈpɛt̬ət̬ɪv/
dangerous /ˈdeɪndʒərəs/
energetic /ˌɛnərˈdʒɛt̬ɪk/
fast /fæst/
hard /hɑrd/
rough /rʌf/

Music
album /ˈælbəm/
band /bænd/
festival /ˈfɛstəvl/
instrument /ˈɪnstrəmənt/
orchestra /ˈɔrkəstrə/
tracks /træks/

Living English
pillow /ˈpɪloʊ/
rhythm /ˈrɪðm/
silent /ˈsaɪlənt/
suitable /ˈsut̬əbl/

Review 5
equipment /ɪˈkwɪpmənt/
hockey /ˈhɑki/
kites /kaɪts/
netball /ˈnɛtbɔl/
protect /prəˈtɛkt/

Unit 6

Business
advertise /ˈædvərtaɪz/
create /kriˈeɪt/
design /dɪˈzaɪn/
research /rɪˈsərtʃ, ˈrisərtʃ/
sell /sɛl/
be successful /ˌbi səkˈsɛsfl/

Public activities
appear /əˈpɪr/
campaign /kæmˈpeɪn/
give a speech /ˌgɪv ə ˈspitʃ/
organize /ˈɔrgənaɪz/
raise money /ˌreɪz ˈmʌni/
set up /ˌsɛt̬ ˈʌp/

Living English
dance routine /ˈdæns ruˌtinʌ/
discouraged /dɪˈskərɪdʒd/
diversity /dəˈvərsət̬i, daɪ-/
gender /ˈdʒɛndər/
inspiration /ˌɪnspəˈreɪʃn/
race /reɪs/
syndrome /ˈsɪndroʊm/
track race /ˈtræk ˌreɪs/

Review 6
injured /'ɪndʒərd/

Magazine 2
achievement /ə'tʃivmənt/
forum /'fɔrəm/
join /ˌdʒɔɪn/

Unit 7

Travel essentials
driver's license /'draɪvərz ˌlaɪsəns/
flip-flops /'flɪp ˌflɑps/
insect spray /'ɪnsɛkt ˌspreɪ/
phrase book /'freɪz ˌbʊk/
scarf /skɑrf/
sunblock /'sʌnblɑk/
vaccination /ˌvæksɪ'neɪʃn/
wind jacket /'wɪnd ˌdʒækət/

Rules
break (rules) /breɪk (rulz)/
bullying /'bʊliɪŋ/
obey (rules) /oʊ'beɪ (rulz)/
respect /rɪ'spɛkt/
strict /strɪkt/
(be) responsible (for) /ˌ(bi) rɪ'spɑnsəbl (fər)/

Living English
budget /'bʌdʒət/
combat pants /'kɑmbæt ˌpænts/
dumb /dʌm/
individuals /ˌɪndə'vɪdʒuəlz/
outfit /'aʊtfɪt/
unfair /ˌʌn'fɛr/

Unit 8

Stages in life
apply (for a job / to a university) /ə'plaɪ (fər ə 'dʒɑb, /tə ə ˌyunə'vərsəṭi/)
buy a house /ˌbaɪ ə 'haʊs/
get married /ˌgɛt 'mærɪd/
graduate /'grædʒueɪt/
have children /hæv 'tʃɪldrən/
open a business /ˌoʊpən ə 'bɪznəs/
retire /rɪ'taɪər/

The environment
alternative energy /ɔl,tərnəṭɪv 'ɛnərdʒi/
extinct /ɪk'stɪŋkt/
garbage /'gɑrbɪdʒ/

population /ˌpɑpyə'leɪʃn/
global warming /ˌgloʊbl 'wɔrmɪŋ/
fossil fuel /'fɑsl ˌfyuəl/
pollution /pə'luʃn/
recycle /ri'saɪkl/

Living English
air traffic controllers /'ɛr ˌtræfɪk kən,troʊlərz/
download /daʊn'loʊd, 'daʊnloʊd/
futurologists /ˌfyutʃə'rɑlədʒɪsts/
portable reader /ˌpɔrtəbl 'ridər/
waterproof /'wɔṭəpruf, 'wɑ-/

Review 8
disappear /ˌdɪsə'pɪr/
gasoline /ˌgæsə'lin, 'gæsəlin/
solve /sɑlv/
survey /'sərveɪ/
technology /tɛk'nɑlədʒi/

Unit 9

TV shows
audience /'ɔdiəns/
audition /ɔ'dɪʃn/
contestant /kən'tɛstənt/
host /hoʊst/
judges /dʒʌdʒɪz/
prize /praɪz/
recording contract /rɪ'kɔrdɪŋ ˌkɑntrækt/
TV viewer /ˌti 'vi ˌvyuər/

Growing up
was bullied /wəz 'bʊlid/
was expelled /wəz ɪk'spɛld/
got into trouble /ˌgɑt ˌɪntə 'trʌbl/
improved /ɪm'pruvd/
were inspired /ˌwər ɪn'spaɪərd/
skipped (classes) /skɪpt ('klæsɪz)/

Living English
career /kə'rɪr/
industry /'ɪndəstri/
manufactured /ˌmænyə'fæktʃərd/

Review 9
assistant /ə'sɪstənt/
conference room /'kɑnfrəns, 'kɑnfərəns ˌrum/

Magazine 3
antelope /'æntəloʊp/
crocodile steak /'krɑkədaɪl ˌsteɪk/
tablets /'tæbləts/
target /'tɑrgɪt/

Unit 10

Relationships
break up with /ˌbreɪk 'ʌp wɪð/
fall in love with /ˌfɔl ɪn 'lʌv wɪð/
get divorced from /ˌgɛt dɪ'vɔrst frəm/
get married to /ˌgɛt 'mærɪd tə/
have an argument with /ˌhæv ən 'ɑrgyumənt wɪð/
make up with /ˌmeɪk 'ʌp wɪð/

Plans and opinions
arrange /ə'reɪndʒ/
can't stand /ˌkænt 'stænd/
decided /də'saɪdɪd/
keep /kip/
mind /maɪnd/
not (be) interested in /ˌnɑt (bi) 'ɪntrəstəd ɪn/
promise /'prɑməs/

Living English
attraction /ə'trækʃn/
clumsy /'klʌmzi/
impressions /ɪm'prɛʃnz/
share /ʃɛr/
signs /saɪnz/
sincerity /sɪn'sɛrəṭi/
trust /trʌst/

Review 10
brand /brænd/
cyberspace /'saɪbər,speɪs/

Unit 11

Sports equipment
cap /kæp/
fins /fɪnz/
gloves /glʌvz/
mask /mæsk/
puck /pʌk/
snorkel /'snɔrkl/
spikes /spaɪks/
stick /stɪk/

Sports words
court /kɔrt/
field /fild/

goal posts /'goʊl ˌpoʊsts/
net /nɛt/
paddle /'pædl/
racket /'rækɪt/
referee /ˌrɛfə'ri/
umpire /'ʌmpaɪər/

Living English
active /'æktɪv/
amateurs /'æmətʃərz/
committee /kə'mɪṭi/
lacrosse /lə'krɑs/
medals /'mɛdlz/

Review 11
method /'mɛθəd/
strategies /'stræṭədʒiz/
strengths /strɛŋθs/
technique /tɛk'nik/
weaknesses /'wiknəsəz, ɪz/

Unit 12

Places
community center /kə'myunəṭi ˌsɛntər/
gated community /'geɪṭɪd kə,myunəṭi/
homeless shelter /'hoʊmləs ˌʃɛltər/
nursing home /'nərsɪŋ ˌhoʊm/
school campus /'skul ˌkæmpəs/
slum /slʌm/

Expressions with *take, make,* and *do*
do exercise /ˌdu 'ɛksərsaɪz/
do volunteer work /ˌdu ˌvɑləntɪər 'wərk/
make friends /ˌmeɪk 'frɛndz/
make a living /ˌmeɪk ə 'lɪvɪŋ/
take part /ˌteɪk 'pɑrt/
take exams /ˌteɪk ɪg'zæmz/

Other
auction /'ɔkʃn/
bid /bɪd/

Review 12
aware /ə'wɛr/

Magazine 4
enemies /'ɛnəmiz/
enter /'ɛntər/
hang out /ˌhæŋ 'aʊt/